PARADISE ERASED

CHRONICLE OF AN EXILE

By

Miguel Ángel Monzón

Grosvenor House
Publishing Limited

This book is published by
Grosvenor House Publishing Ltd
Link House
140 The Broadway, Tolworth, Surrey, KT6 7HT.
www.grosvenorhousepublishing.co.uk

A CIP record for this book
is available from the British Library

Paperback ISBN 978-1-80381-429-2
Hardback ISBN 978-1-80381-430-8
eBook ISBN 978-1-80381-431-5

This book is based on real life events. The names of a number of individuals
have been changed to protect those still living and who may not wish to be
identified. The author has exercised his own criteria to propel the narrative,
using his personal recollection of events as well as including input from third
parties who participated in the story.

*For my mother, who continues
to fight injustice to this day.*

CONTENTS

CHAPTER 1

The Darkness

Early February, 1977

Viewed from the sky, the city of Santa Marta sparkled like a fistful of diamonds under a silvery moon. A few hours earlier, a gigantic red-tinted sun had disappeared from view above the Caribbean Sea, setting the sky ablaze in deep tones of purple and blue. A breeze descending from the Sierra Nevada shook rows of palm and trupillo trees until their movement resembled a wild dance of nature against the night sky. The first stirrings of the carnival season had drowned out the chirping of the cicadas, and the thumping sound of tropical music reverberated throughout every nook and cranny of the old quarter, where every available space was filled with spectators watching street dancers and where hired serenaders entertained throngs of tourists cramming El Camellón, a bustling promenade delineating a stretch of coast where four-and-a-half centuries ago a fleet of Spanish colonisers had first arrived to the sound of waves crashing against a sandy shore. Masses of revellers raised their voices even louder whilst they drank rum and watched the frenetic spectacle of colourfully costumed dance troupes moving to the rhythm of drums.

An SUV vehicle with tinted windows moved unnoticed through the crowded streets, slowly inching its way past taverns crammed with locals, street vendors and tourists. The driver bore the serenity of someone who had been trained to avoid arousing the slightest suspicion. Sitting next to him was a slim man in his thirties and in the back of the vehicle four other men, who now felt able to exchange a few words.

"There was nothing left in the other car, was there?"

"Nothing ... All spick and span."

The vehicle moved faster as it drew away from the city centre. The individual who asked the initial question, and answered to the name of Jason, closed his eyes and dried the sweat from his brow, the events of the last three hours projecting from the back of his mind as the vehicle advanced more quickly towards the outskirts of the city and the hum of street music grew increasingly intermittent. The sound of a woman's screams echoed inside his head, interspersed with still vivid scenes that had taken place just minutes before in an apartment. He recalled her desperate struggle to free herself from the grip of the men forcing themselves onto her against a marble floor. The flashbacks felt like an eternity to him, until they were interrupted by the sound of the car radio. A crackling news bulletin announced a forthcoming meeting between the Colombian president, Alfonso López Michelsen and his USA counterpart, Gerald Ford.

The SUV continued to course at high speed along a freeway devoid of traffic and illuminated by a seemingly endless row of amber lights. Suddenly, it took an abrupt turn and, leaving the asphalted road, drove through dry, dusty bushes at the side. The unpaved, uneven terrain led to an unlit, stony area, where the car finally came to a stop some twenty meters away from a nearby hill.

The light of the full moon was bright enough for the six men not to need their torches. The first one, who seemed to be their leader, cast a circular glance over the expanse of bare land. His untucked white shirt gave him ready access to the gun he carried concealed in the front of his trousers. Another of them opened the boot of the car and pulled out an electric saw from a toolbox.

Jason unzipped the end of the bag with trembling fingers, exposing a girl's face. Her open eyes seemed to be staring directly at him.

"If you're going to get jittery, then step aside" admonished the leader, "because we need to get busy. Just make sure there's nothing left in the boot."

The other three lifted the body bag from the back of the car and proceeded to carry it towards a hillside. This was the place that the planners amongst them had designated as the most suitable spot for the grim business of disappearing the body: a conveniently remote area where nobody was likely to hear the echoing noise of a chainsaw. The members of the group were no strangers to carrying out tasks of a similar nature, with the exception of the newer participant who appeared to be ill at ease with his assignment. The tall, slim man, who had earlier rebuked his colleague, watched his nervy associate and shook his head

"I knew he didn't have the guts for this", he said to the other two in a resigned tone.

"We've been assured he's very meticulous when it comes to cleaning up", interjected another member of the group as his colleagues dropped the bag containing the young woman's body onto the ground beside a deep shaft in the hillside.

"Every cloud has a silver lining", muttered the tall man, in an attempt to infuse the macabre occasion with some kind of normality as he watched the most determined of his colleagues dismember the girl's body with the saw. Another member of the team, wearing gloves, carefully gathered the portions and dropped them into the shaft that at some other time had served as a cistern for collecting rainwater.

The men then proceeded to empty the plastic containers of corrosive acid down onto the pieces of dismembered body now lying at the bottom of the shaft. Caustic fumes emanating from the shaft rose up the hillside, ascending uninterrupted towards the very heavens.

CHAPTER 2

The Bubble

Mid-October, 1976

The oval candle at the centre of the huge birthday cake was shaped like a number eight and stood red and shiny as a tomato just a few centimetres from my face.

Flanking the enormous cake on the table, as if they had been entrusted with the task of guarding it, were neat rows of cylindrical paper soldiers, each containing an assortment of sweets and all wearing blue-and-red military uniforms. Alongside the soldiers was a small group of handmade Pierrot-style clowns in pointy paper hats.

My classmates grouped themselves around the big table in the living room of my house, all singing happy birthday. Anticipation had caused a swarm of butterflies to flutter endlessly in my belly. When the key moment came, I extinguished the lonely flame above the red candle with a single puff. During the deafening applause that erupted, time seemed to stop for a few seconds as I stood motionless contemplating the slim trail of paraffin smoke rising all the way to the ceiling.

It might seem like stating the obvious but the day of my birthday was definitely the event I most looked forward to every year since I had developed a sense of self. There simply was no substitute to having all my classmates gathered in one place celebrating with me.

From my earliest memory, mum always asked me well in advance what kind of cake I wished to have. On one occasion, I requested a cake in the shape of a castle, on another a ship adorned with chimneys pumping out clouds made of sugar. This year, I told her I wanted a cake as big as the wheel of a truck.

For the occasion, I wore new patent leather shoes, a formal short-sleeved shirt patterned with a nautical design, a stamped blue tie and my hair combed to the right.

Suddenly, the stern voice of one of our female school teachers urged all my classmates to form an orderly queue. Two ladies from our school, one

4

who was our geography teacher and the other who taught us arithmetic, had offered to help mother keep things running smoothly at home. However, it was widely acknowledged that San Isidro de Toledo, our primary school, enjoyed the reputation of teaching the most orderly and obedient children in the city.

My mother emerged from the kitchen, wearing a smile that seemed to radiate light all around her. Dressed for the occasion with modest elegance, she placed the utensils on the table and began slicing the huge cake in equal portions, placing each piece on a white cardboard plate.

"Ladies first! And then the gentlemen!" Mother announced, whilst proceeding to minister to the children standing in line.

The day of my birthday was also the day I chose to celebrate my mother as the axis of my universe and the calm at the centre of any storm. Perplexingly, and despite my having just turned eight, she still insisted on spoiling me as if I was five years old.

Her name was Carmen and she was a woman of simple habits, typical of those of her generation who with tenacity and hard effort had managed to overcome all manner of adversity. For me, mother was a force of nature that kept everything in balance, a being possessed of an innate ability to dispel feelings of anguish and despondency with nothing more than her presence.

The very first question I remember asking her was: "Mom, where does the rain come from and where does it go?". It was then that she taught me one of life's most valuable lessons, forceful in its simplicity: that nothing is ever lost. Just like the rain that falls from the sky, everything in life has a constant and defined cycle; that, with mathematical precision, each river returns to its riverbed and everything eventually reaches its destination; and so the cycle closes, encapsulating the natural order of things. It was a natural law that could be effectively applied to every aspect of life. As a result, I revelled in the certainty and orderliness of the world that I was living in.

When all school activity ceased for a couple of days a week, mother and I would travel to her farm away from the city, where I would spend my time listening to the sound of rushing streams descending from misty mountains, breathing the fresh air and drinking warm, fresh milk in the chill of early mornings.

Alternatively, on occasions I spent at my grandmother's house, the afternoon sun would often find me lying on high branches of fruit trees, notebook in hand, classifying all kinds of fauna in her huge backyard and contemplating for hours at a time the trajectory of clouds that would whimsically transform into faces or fancifully assume the shape of fantastical creatures.

I had finally succeeded in conquering my fear of school. The large two-storey house that welcomed us all daily with open arms had become an enriching part of my general routine. Not only did I know each one of my thirty classmates by name, I was also familiar with their individual quirks and the particular sound of their voices. We learned the same school songs and participated in the same games under the sun or in the shade of lush trees in the large courtyard of our primary school, helping us to forge close and long-lasting ties of union.

My mother had carefully selected the school not because it was the most popular or the most expensive. She had done so in the certainty that at San Isidro de Toledo I would find the most nurturing environment for my development as a responsible member of society.

The rousing school anthem we sang every morning before class was a poem set to music, an open invitation to drink from springs of knowledge, and none of us harboured the faintest doubt that we were all headed for a glorious destiny. For we were not just the youth of the future. We were the future engineers, doctors, judges and lawyers. We were the citizens of tomorrow.

For now, we were all living an idyllic everlasting suspended in time, every aspect of our short existence permeated by an abundant sense of innocence and naivety.

A turntable in a corner of the room provided low-volume background music while we made the cake disappear with copious amounts of sweet sparkling soda. Little by little, the sound of the voices in the room grew in intensity as the disposable plates and glasses we had used began to pile up; these in turn were dutifully collected and carried to the kitchen by Manuela, our part-time housekeeper.

We then gathered together as a group by a large window in the living room, which offered an almost uninterrupted view of the garden outside. We then witnessed the spectacle of dozens of soap bubbles rising up to the sky, driven by a mild afternoon breeze and reflecting the dying rays of the sun in multicoloured tones that, for the space of an hour, infused the air with a golden radiance.

In the meantime, Tamara Escovedo Jordan, a tall elegant woman of delicate features, founder and principal of our school, widely regarded as one of the most enterprising and respected figures of the educational community in the country, stood positioned in a corner of the room with her camera, busily taking photographs of the event, flanked by her two daughters, both of whom had the insufferable habit of tickling me during school breaks.

Exhausted but happy, the afternoon saw me handing out paper clowns and artisan French soldiers to each one of my guests who, with hair covered with confetti, were now heading out to board the sky blue school bus waiting outside the house with the engine running. While our principal spoke to my mum, her daughters took turns to hug me by way of farewell. The colour of our school bus was exactly the same as the colour of our uniforms, closely resembling the blue sky that we looked at every morning from our passenger windows as we were driven to class.

I stood alone on the terrace, waving frantically at my classmates who were all smiles on the bus as they returned animated farewell gestures from their windows. One of them crossed his eyes and wrote the number eight on the glass by licking it with his tongue. There's always one, I thought.

As the vehicle, loaded with pupils and teachers, slowly disappeared into the distance, I turned my attention to the employee who was still blowing soap bubbles in the garden of the house. It was still sunny under the Caribbean skies and the last rays of the day were keeping alive the multicoloured show of floating spheres.

When you haven't accumulated as many miles on the clock as most adults, life has a tendency to flash before your eyes at the most inopportune moments. Back then, the gamut of my life experience was confined to a handful of carefully mapped out activities which included trips to school and weekend forays to our dairy and poultry farm on the outskirts of the city.

I fixed my eyes on the last of the soap bubbles still defying gravity among the leaves of the trees, a silvery orb constantly changing shape and reflecting the full colour spectrum of everything around it until I convinced myself that fragments from my short life were being projected onto the bubble's silvery surface, gliding in a carefree bounce across the garden.

"This is your life" I thought to myself, as I visualised myself in grandma's backyard, resting on the thick branch of a plum tree, deep in concentration and drawing with a pencil on a notebook to the sound of wild birds singing as the branches gently swayed in the afternoon breeze.

Once again the bubble was tossed around by a capricious change in the direction of the wind and there I was again, casting my mind to moments spent at my mother's farm near the Sierra Nevada, our weekend retreat from the hustle and bustle of city life. I could feel the pungent aroma of manure invading my nostrils whilst I drank steaming fresh milk from a pitcher early in the morning and fed corn to flocks of chicken to the murmur of nearby cascading springs. I think the most confrontational I ever got with my mother was when, having formed an attachment with a number of cows at the farm, I became aware of where the meat on our table had been coming from. I therefore made her swear to me under oath that no further slaughtering of cattle was ever to take place at the farm and that henceforth our cows were to be allowed to live out their natural lives in peace, a request that to mother's everlasting credit she duly complied with.

I saw my reflection in the bubble and more fragments of my life flashed before my eyes, such as emerging from the blue school bus in my blue uniform at the end of a long day and running towards the arms of my mother, who like clockwork was there to greet me at the front door of our house, my own private fortress and the setting of my earliest memories.

Surrounded by a feeling of tranquility like dew descending upon my face, I paused to reflect on my good fortune and on the protective bubble that enveloped and nurtured my existence: the protective sphere that, with meticulous effort and dedication, my mother had managed to construct around me. A sphere of stability and permanence that repelled all harm, a bubble unaltered by any winds of change or everyday vicissitudes and where certainty and security were the only constants in life.

Suddenly and without warning, however, the bubble symbolising the stability of my world would explode silently before my startled gaze, as if it had never existed.

CHAPTER 3

The Tourist

Mid November, 1976

It is Friday, 12th November, 1976, approximately 11:30 in the morning. A couple of hands are fast at work on a typewriter, the noise of the machine's keys drowned out by the cacophony of frenzied activity unfolding within an office complex, where a dozen people can be seen walking hastily across the main hub of desks and up and down the narrow corridors. Others sit talking on the phone or communicating loudly with one another across the room. This organised chaos takes place under a huge propeller fan circulating stale hot air around the approximately 150 square meters of office space, composed of a series of work units subdivided by screens. This comprises the operations centre of the branch of state police known as the F-2.

Outside the headquarters, 13th Street in Santa Marta is a bustling urban environment under the shadow of the Casa Consistorial, an imposing sixteenth-century building where City Hall operates, its balconied rear part dominating a narrow passageway where fruit vendors and merchants such as Forero the paraplegic shoe-cleaner do what they can to earn a living. The main thoroughfare is dotted with a series of re-purposed colonial-style houses, coffee houses and soda fountains, where correspondents from local radio stations and newspaper columnists occupy vantage points, clutching ice cold drinks to ward off the heat, eager for a scoop or just hoping to get the latest gossip while keeping a watchful eye for the arrival of any detainees being brought into custody.

Inside the compound, two policemen dressed in civilian clothes burst through the main entrance and approached the reception area, bringing with them a young man in handcuffs who can be seen struggling slightly. Alongside them is a tall blonde girl, twenty-seven years of age, showing confusion on her face and reacting to the busy and unfamiliar environment with anxiety and discomfort.

9

At that precise moment, Carmen stepped out of her office, which was located by a back corridor at the opposite end of the police department building. The first person she noticed was this tall young woman in the vicinity of the reception, looking around in a visible state of distress. Carmen also caught a glimpse of a boy in counterfeit sports clothing being restrained by two police officers, one of them called Vergara and the other known to everyone as Cabo Valverde.

The young woman focused on Carmen, realising she was the only other female visible in the predominantly male environment. Slowly, but with determination, the girl approached the officer. She had the complexion of someone whose skin was not used to being exposed to too much sunlight. She wore high-quality summer clothes and had no belongings on her except a small book she held in her hand.

Almost in slow motion, the two women approached one another through the other passers-by, until they were face to face. Carmen instinctively addressed the girl with words of reassurance before realising she didn't understand Spanish very well. In turn, the young tourist tried to make herself understood with rudimentary words and hand gestures.

"I have no documentation… I have no money… I am a tourist…"

Urgently browsing through the small book she was carrying, which turned out to be a small Spanish pocket dictionary, the young woman pointed in the direction of the suspect:

"That boy, with two others… they stole my camera and my bag and left me without any money, without my passport, without my camera, without anything…"

In a closed office away from the hustle and bustle of the F-2 headquarters, Carmen turned on a portable electric fan on an archive cabinet, pointing in the direction of the woman, who was sitting at a large oval table in the middle of the room. She then turned her attention to a piece of paper the tourist had scribbled on.

"Your name is Georgiana Ellis-Carrington, a British national travelling on her own?"

"That's right. I am." She offered the girl a drink of water in a paper cup. Pulling up a chair, Carmen sat next to her and watched her drink the contents of the cup. Without warning, the young woman started to hyperventilate. The officer looked at her for a few seconds before calming her down with slow hand gestures.

"You've just had a traumatic experience. But I can assure you that from now on you are going to feel much better. Now please take a deep breath, along with me, and try to hold it in for a few seconds before emptying your lungs. Like this…"

The young woman quietly acquiesced and followed suit. They performed the exercise several times before Carmen spoke again:

"I was a nurse years ago. They taught us how to do this to calm people's nerves."

"I practise yoga…", said the girl. "I think chanting also helps".

"Great! We've got this!" smiled Carmen, and the two women realised they had managed to overcome the language barrier. Georgiana glanced around the room surrounded by grey metal cabinets under the cold glare of twin halogen lights in the ceiling.

"I hope you feel comfortable here despite the gloomy lighting", Carmen said. "I would have taken you to my office… but it's a bit claustrophobic and the hottest place on earth! And there's no electric fan. We probably have more fresh air here than anywhere else in the building!"

Opening her expressive eyes, the girl answered with a melodic tone of voice: "Yes, like in the Sierra Nevada! The air there is very pure!"

Carmen laughed, and nodded in agreement: "You are absolutely right! And it took a tourist like yourself to remind me of a few home truths!"

"I took some very good photographs in Ciudad Perdida…", added the young woman: "But those images are gone now, with my camera!"

Suddenly remembering why they were there in the first place, Carmen pulled out a notebook and a pen. "This is the part where I have to ask you some questions about what happened to you out there. Can you tell me exactly how many attackers there were?"

Moments later, Carmen sat face-to-face with the young man in the sports T-shirt, who looked visibly perturbed. They were in the fingerprinting department, a confined area of the hub separated from other office cubicles by a perspex screen.

"There were three of us," replied the suspect, while she took notes with a pen.

"I was shouting 'Help'" the young foreigner had explained to Carmen in the secluded filing-cabinet office, availing herself of her dictionary. "when two men… dressed in civilian clothes… came out of nowhere and started chasing the boys. Those two got away… but they captured the boy who was still holding me…"

11

"But it's so difficult for us to make an honest living…" the dejected suspect in the enclosure of the office hub muttered in a remorseful tone. "Sometimes we just don't know how we're going to survive from one day to the next…". He closed his eyes and rested his head on his chest.

Carmen nodded in silence as she continued to take notes.

Two agents came and led him away from the office hub, still handcuffed, towards the detention cells in the back yard. Carmen looked on from her seat with an air of sadness.

As her last duty of the day, Carmen found herself in the confines of her small office typing up copious notes on her trusty Olivetti typewriter. Reviewing the two separate statements of the young woman and her assailant, she tried not to think too much about the teenager she had interviewed moments earlier, before finally putting the paperwork in a metal closet in the archives office where she had been with the tourist. Prior to joining the F-2, Carmen had worked for the military at the Córdova Fifth Infantry Battalion, where she had acquired the habit of making duplicates of every document that passed through her hands. Having filed away the copies of the statements in the personal file she kept in her office, she turned to a photo of me as a smiling chubby-cheeked toddler on her desk and thought about how nice it would be to be back home to keep me company.

It was still a sunny and bright early evening when she finally emerged from the headquarters. Sitting on a wooden box, surrounded by the paraphernalia of his craft was Forero, the swarthy middle-aged paraplegic who, despite having lost the use of his legs due to polio, earned a living polishing shoes. He gestured at Carmen from across the street and she waved back at Forero and as usual asked him if he needed anything. Stopping a street vendor carrying fresh fruit on a wheelbarrow, she paid for her usual bag of oranges and exchanged a few pleasantries with the merchant before driving back home from Plaza de San Francisco with a brown paper bag full of oranges on the passenger seat while a bolero song from the car radio played in the background.

Meanwhile, alone in her hotel room, Georgiana got out of her bed, where she had been idling the hours away reminiscing on the day's events, and ambled towards her balcony with its almost uninterrupted view of El Morro, Santa Marta's islet in the middle of the ocean. Lost in thought, she watched the gleaming sea and the multicoloured spectacle of a sky set aflame by the dying light of a setting sun.

CHAPTER 4

The Bells

Mid November 1976, three days later

A large group of pigeons scattered in unison in the vicinity of Santa Marta's Basilica the moment the bells started to toll early in the morning. The historic centre came to life from streetsellers advertising their hot black coffee, freshly squeezed orange juice, morning papers and lottery tickets. Mounds of orange peel and pineapple skin began to accumulate in municipal containers all along Fifth Street while pedestrians tried to negotiate their way to work along the city's busiest thoroughfare.

It was Monday morning of 15th November. As usual, Carmen was one of the first members of staff to arrive at the police department, where the sound of the ceiling fan competed with the humming of the air conditioner from the nearby office of the chief of police. Part of her early morning ritual included sharing her morning coffee from her thermos flask and a little conversation with several of her colleagues in the office hub of the F-2 before walking to her office in a long corridor that led to a storage area for confiscated goods. The corridor continued on to a patio housing detention cells.

As a rule, and before the usual deluge of incoming calls began, Carmen spent no more than two minutes on the phone to check I had got to school while looking at the framed picture of me on her desk. Having exchanged a few reassuring words with the school office, she then called our housekeeper to ensure all necessary errands were being carried out before replacing the handset.

Glancing casually across the dimly lit corridor outside her office, Carmen noticed that the door leading to the room that housed the official archives was slightly ajar. She was aware that designated members of staff had access to the facility during working hours and so the unlocked door was not an unusual occurrence in itself. However, guided by an instinct she could not fathom, she left her office and walked across the corridor towards the door, turning on the spotlights as she entered the room. She approached one of the metal storage cabinets stacked against the wall and opened a drawer. Flicking through the files that had been processed during the past week, she singled out the folder of documents from the previous Friday. To her surprise, the statement she had taken from the teenage assailant Diego Alberto Jesus Díaz was nowhere to be found – and neither was the reference number she had allocated to that same declaration. Instead, she found an older file on the suspect, rubber-stamped with the words "In Progress", which made no mention of his detention of three days ago, when she had watched him being led away in handcuffs to the cells in the back yard.

Swallowing dry, she browsed once more through the pages of the same documents, this time more thoroughly. Then she checked the nearby folders. But she failed to find any record of the young man's arrest.

Placing the documents back in their cabinet, she made sure she left the papers exactly as she had found them and closed the cabinet drawer. Returning to her office, she accessed her personal file. As she had expected, she found her photocopies of the original declaration that she had taken the precaution of making and archiving for herself the previous Friday, just before the end of her weekly shift. Not only did the copy in her hands contain Diego Alberto's details, but a cursory look at the document also confirmed the day of his arrest as well as the date stamp on his recorded statement.

Having locked her office behind her, she went to the open door onto the back yard, directing her gaze at the detention cells, which were essentially bare dungeons partially exposed to the elements. The cells were all empty, which wasn't unusual on Monday mornings, as the lack of running water and toilet facilities in the cells made it illegal for the police to hold detainees for more than 48 hours at a time. Before the end of that decade, the nation had yet to institute a judicial branch of Government to prosecute offenders or review judicial processes. There were no appointed Attorney Generals to investigate crimes or review judicial processes to minimise the continuous backlog of cases growing exponentially, a situation exacerbated by a relentless and very public armed vendetta between the notorious Cárdenas and Valdeblánquez clans which was then unfolding in various regions of the Atlantic Coast.

Before Carmen could organize her thoughts, she became aware of a disturbance in the office hub, resonating increasingly throughout the building. It was the voice of a woman shouting at the top of her lungs.

"Where is my son? I want to see him! What have you done with my Diego? Radio bulletins have been reporting he's been detained here since last Friday! I want some answers, please let me go!"

As Carmen ran through the corridor towards the office hub, she encountered an irate but mostly desperate-looking woman of about forty years of age, with mangled dyed hair, multicoloured clothing, plastic bangles on her wrists and a counterfeit gold chain with trinkets around her neck, advancing towards the reception area.

Matilde Andrade was a single mother who lived in a curious boat-shaped house built on dry land that served as accommodation for her and her six children in the northern sector of Pescaíto, from where she supplemented her meagre income by selling homemade love potions and doing Tarot card readings for anybody willing to pay the fee.

Today, while attempting to force her way through a group of F-2 officials, Matilde made it clear in no uncertain terms that she would refuse to leave the premises until she had been informed of her son's whereabouts.

"I've just talked to three journalists at the soda fountain across the street and they tell me you have dungeons at the back of this precinct... So, if my son's not there now, where on earth are you keeping him?"

While she was still speaking, two F-2 enforcement officers rushed forward and pushed her face down onto a nearby desk to immobilise her, though she continued to struggle:

"Take your hands off me, you sons of bitches!!!"

Carmen, who up until that moment had been a petrified spectator of the unfolding spectacle, lunged towards the desk where the two police officers were forcibly restraining the woman. Shouting out loud, she frantically attempted to prise the agents away from Matilde:

"There's no need for any of this!... Please get off her!... Don't you dare hurt this poor woman!"

In that instant, José Francisco Carrasco, head of the F-2, emerged from his office in a furious rage. Coming to a stop at the end of the corridor, the lieutenant shouted with a voice that made the walls tremble:

"What the hell is going on here?"

All activity in the office hub ceased immediately and almost absolute silence prevailed, interrupted only by the noise of the electric fan blades.

An hour later, half a dozen individuals quietly sat around the large oval table in the archives office. The scene was so tense it could be cut with a knife. All eyes focused on Lieutenant José Francisco Carrasco, with his ruddy complexion and round face, who quietly observed the group from his seat, meeting everyone's gaze while tapping the surface of the table with his fingers. Sitting next to him was his right-hand man, Valverde, tall and thin, with a penetrating stare and a face devoid of any sign of human emotion. Alongside him was Sarmiento, alias "El Totumo" ['the Calabash'], a small, shifty individual in his early thirties with roving eyes, lacquered hair, wearing a checked shirt. In the seat next to him was Vergara, alias "Espuela" ['Spur'], of white complexion and a vacant expression. At the opposite end of the oval table sat the young tourist, who had been brought in to the premises from her hotel accommodation by agents. Matilde and Carmen occupied seats next to her.

Breaking the silence, Carrasco addressed the young woman with a tone of forced courtesy, his intonation deliberately slow but sharp and clear:

"We have convened this meeting so that you may help us establish an accurate description of a certain suspect accompanying the robber who assaulted you and took your belongings. We understand that you managed to get a good look at him before he fled the scene."

Dictionary in hand, Georgiana proceeded to speak in a melodic foreign accent:

"I was taking pictures of the beach with my camera... close to the sea port... Suddenly, my camera was snatched away from my hands ... The next thing I felt was a push on the side that knocked me to the ground... this other boy grabbed my purse and ran away along with another friend who I couldn't see very well. But I did get a good look at the boy who grabbed my purse... he was a thin young man in his teens, with dark complexion and straight hair. He wasn't wearing any shoes and wore a dark blue T-shirt... with two horizontal white lines and the logo of a yellow crocodile on it"

Touching the area above her right eyebrow, she added: "He also had a scar on one side of his forehead".

"Matilde's son... tried to keep me pinned down on the floor... At that moment I saw these two gentlemen arrive..." Georgiana looked at Vergara and Valverde "They came running to where we were while I was shouting for help... they were wearing civilian clothes, just like they are today... I didn't know they were police..."

The agents sitting around the table stared at her without comment. The stale air circulated by the electric fan tossed her long hair from side to side.

16

The young woman then looked at Matilde and continued: "They threw themselves on the boy… handcuffed him immediately… and in a matter of minutes we were all in this building… As for the other two boys… they managed to get away…" Turning to Carmen, she concluded: "This is a lengthier version of the statement I gave this lady last Friday…"

When she had finished speaking, those sitting around the oval table looked on in silence while others jotted away on their notebooks. Sitting stock still in his chair, Valverde watched her impassively.

The first person to break the silence was Sarmiento, alias "El Totumo", the group's official gatherer of rumours and possessor of up-to-date knowledge of local families living in the city's deprived areas, particularly those harbouring youngsters with criminal records. He addressed the group like someone about to pull a rabbit out of a hat.

"Lieutenant, I think the young lady has given us a useful description of a certain individual well-known to my contacts. Details such as the counterfeit LaCoste T-shirt and the scar on the forehead sound familiar to me. And if that is indeed the case, then we could do a lot worse than paying a visit to that neighbourhood, and, if what shines is gold, then we can be certain of nabbing Boquita's partner in crime." (Matilde's son was known as 'Boquita' and referring to individuals by their nickname was a common regional custom).

"I don't have a problem with that," Carrasco assented almost disinterestedly with a wave of his hand. "And if the rest of the group is in agreement, then I have no issue with organising a search team immediately. Sarmiento will be in charge of the operation. If we are indeed dealing with Diego Alberto's accomplice then it's time we brought him here to ask him a few questions."

"Let it never be said that we do not look after our citizens' rights, including those of our tourists", ventured Arango, the team's designated driver.

"And satisfied tourists bring even more tourists", concluded Cristancho, whose salient features were his facial scars and the habit of wanting to finish everybody's sentences during conversation.

Suddenly, Matilde Andrade, who throughout the entire process had quietly been sitting next to the young tourist, exploded with rage:

"I've been sitting here like an idiot watching your pantomime for what seems like an eternity and I'm still not hearing anything regarding my son's whereabouts or what you have done with him!"

With an air of exasperation, Lieutenant Carrasco turned to admonish the woman: "I suggest you leave this matter in the hands of the authorities. That's us. In the meantime, please keep quiet while you are in this room!"

Matilde retorted even more angrily: "Don't you dare lecture me while you and your useless gang of layabouts still haven't told me what has happened to my son!"

With an air of disdain, Carrasco responded: "Well, quite frankly, none of us in here is obliged to put up with your shouting and abuse any longer. Cabo, show her the door."

Taking his cue, Valverde stood up and proceeded to forcibly remove Matilde from the office, despite the woman's loud protestations. Visibly upset by the scene, Carmen exhaled, closing her eyes with an air of helplessness and disgust.

At that very moment, and while everyone around the table was momentarily distracted by the scene, Carmen felt Georgiana's hand closing around her wrist.

"I can't stay at the hotel any longer" Georgiana spoke up, "nor do I have any means of withdrawing funds without my documents."

When she saw the agents' eyes all focusing on her, she stopped talking. With a forced smile, Lieutenant Carrasco adopted a sudden tone of benevolence, assuring her that everything was under control.

"You have nothing to worry about. As you can see we are all here at your service."

He took a few steps towards the women and addressed Carmen. "Would you be willing to grant this charming young lady temporary accommodation in your house until we resolve her situation?"

Given the urgency of the situation, and feeling a sense of responsibility towards the dejected looking girl, Carmen responded without hesitation.

"Yes, I will take care of her. She's more than welcome to stay in my house."

"Excellent. That's settled, then", concluded. "Okay boys, time to get going."

When they had left the room, Carmen spoke to Georgiana in a low voice in a bid to calm her nerves: "Don't worry. I'll make sure I settle anything you have outstanding at the hotel. Then I'll take you shopping so we can get any little things you might need. Afterwards, if you feel like it, we'll grab a quick meal. You are more than welcome to stay in my house until your situation is resolved. You're going to be quite comfortable there."

It was quite late at night when I was awakened by the sound of an engine outside and light filtering through my bedroom curtains. I jumped out of bed, and parting the drapes just enough to see mum's car coming to a stop in front of the house. I had been sent to bed shortly after supper by the housekeeper, who had told me mother would be coming home late. Right at that moment, I felt it was never late enough to rush to meet mum and give her a welcome hug. The truth was I had missed her presence in the house all evening.

I left my room in my light blue pyjamas without turning on the lights, and walked barefoot along the corridor that led to our living room just in time to see the glow of the terrace light as the front door opened. However, I came to an abrupt stop when I heard two contrasting tones of voice, one of them familiar, the other totally unknown to me.

I immediately hid behind a column by the dining room, from where I could glimpse the silhouette of two women. Carrying in her hand what looked like a large shopping bag, mum muttered something unintelligible in a low voice before switching on one of the table lamps, its light bathing the room with a golden glow.

"Please make yourself at home. I'll show you to your room shortly, but in the meantime let me squeeze some oranges. Would you like your juice with or without ice?"

"Without ice for me, thank you."

The crystalline, musical tone of the unknown voice made me think of the sound of singing. The figure of a woman wearing a pink veranera blouse and denim trousers came into my field of vision and stopped in the middle of the room. As she looked around herself, her long hair reflected the light of the lamp like the glow of a new dawn.

I momentarily lost sight of her as she continued to walk slowly across the room and so I shifted my position behind the column accordingly in order to observe her more closely. She seemed distracted by a series of small family portraits on a dresser. Reaching for one of the portraits, she brought it close to her face. It was a photo of me. From that particular angle, the glass cover of the portrait reflected the area behind her, my location by the column now exposed by the dim light in the room. She turned her head in my direction, looking straight into my eyes. My cover blown, I backtracked in silence along the corridor, still keeping an eye on the lounge area until I was again concealed by the darkness. With a feeling of embarrassment but suddenly very eager for the next day to arrive, I quietly returned to my room, thinking of the unexpected golden apparition who seemed to have come straight out of a fairy tale.

CHAPTER 5

The Maiden

Mid November, 1976

I would be lying if I said I managed to get a proper night's sleep. Rather, I spent what seemed like endless hours moving from side to side in my bed, impatiently waiting to drift into sleep. After my morning shower, I got dressed and dragged myself in my school uniform all the way to the dining room to join mother at the table for breakfast. Sitting in one of the chairs was the woman from the previous night, resplendent in broad daylight, as if her presence in our house was the most natural occurrence in the world. Mum offered me a different chair from my usual one and sat between us. I struggled to remain calm and appear normal.

"*Buenos días*", I say without directing my eyes to anyone in particular.

"*Buenos días*", replies the maiden from the fairytale while out of the corner of my eye I detect a faint smile on her face.

Aware of my confusion, mum tilts her head towards me: "Miguel Ángel, this is Georgiana. She knows very little Spanish. She will be spending a few days with us in our house".

I suddenly realise the woman in our midst might actually be real, albeit from a totally different world. While furtively looking at her in the morning glare, I am somewhat reminded of the plastic dolls that my grandmother keeps in a storage room at the back of her big yellow house, along with dusty boxes of phonograph records and other nostalgic paraphernalia, childhood dolls that once upon a time might have belonged to her defunct older sister, with their round plastic faces and ruddy pink cheeks, unfeasibly large blue eyes and synthetic golden hair. I allow myself a steadier look at the flesh-and-blood apparition at our table, who also has blue eyes, pink cheeks and golden hair. More remarkably still, the soft features and overall aura of the woman are oddly reminiscent of something else altogether.

Before I am able to pursue that thought, mashed green bananas with scrambled eggs arrive, courtesy of Manuela the housekeeper. The women become engaged in the most curious and animated of conversations, so much so that neither notices when I move to the other end of the table and open my school bag to retrieve my sketchbook. Grabbing a pencil, I begin to sketch the scene before my eyes, paying particular attention to the gesticulating apparition who moves her hands frantically while speaking in a decidedly odd accent.

"I did the Inca Trail... My goal was to see Machu Picchu high up on the Andes... you have to be physically fit... Afterwards I took a bus from Cuzco to the capital and flew to Bogotá, which was just as cold and rainy as it is back home... and then came on here to Santa Marta... I didn't want to miss the ruins of Ciudad Perdida near the Sierra Nevada..."

"I worked for the army before joining the police force..." my mum explains, and I reflect on the novel oddity of hearing her speaking Spanish so slowly. "But I trained as a nurse way before all that... By some quirk of fate, I delivered babies in the same hospital where I was born!"

While the women are telling each other their life stories, I sketch busily on a page in my book in an attempt to catch the moment, drawing the outline of the stranger's face before concentrating on the animated movement of her hands, ending up with markings ultimately resembling the haphazard trajectory of a dozen doves in flight.

Right on cue, the blue school bus signals its presence outside the house with a sound of its horn, so off I run, bag in hand, without so much as a goodbye.

Our school was a large repurposed two-storey house on a corner of Avenida del Libertador, the city's longest and most transited road. The building featured a rectangular front garden and contained eight classrooms inside. On the top floor there was the religious education room, where I sit quietly at the back fully engaged in completing from memory a more detailed drawing of the facial features I had earlier observed on the tourist sitting at our dining table. To say that I am distracted would be an understatement. I am completely unaware that the teacher in charge of the class has painstakingly written the Apostles Creed on the chalkboard for us to copy into our notebooks. Nor am I fazed when the entire class starts reciting the text in unison. The class falls silent when the teacher suddenly motions them to stop, grabs an eraser, and wipes the board clean.

"Miguel Ángel. Would you be good enough to stand up and recite the Apostles Creed so that the rest of us can hear it? It appears you find drawing on your own far more preferable to learning alongside your fellow pupils."

I dutifully stand up, thinking of all the evenings grandma had spent coaching me from an early age until I had memorised every conceivable prayer ever devised by the Catholic Church. Taking a deep breath, I reel off the entire prayer in a mechanical, dispassionate manner:

"I believe in God, the Father Almighty, Creator of Heaven and Earth; and in Jesus Christ, His only Son, Our Lord, … I believe in the Holy Spirit, the holy Catholic Church, the communion of saints, the forgiveness of sins, the resurrection of the body and life everlasting…"

Absolute silence dominates the room. I observe the girl next to me elbowing her companion while the teacher glowers in my direction with gritted teeth.

The school bell then rings and, while our teacher is still addressing the class in the middle of the din, we grab our bags and march downstairs to our next lesson, like uniformed cadets.

It had come to the attention of teachers that, as a norm, students had a low tolerance threshold for certain academic subjects. In order to liven up the class and aid our learning by keeping us all attentive during lessons, our history teacher had devised a novel method of teaching, involving the use of props and role play, and everyone receiving an assignment was encouraged to "re-live the moment" before the entire class. As the first step, the teacher draws the outline of a large door on the chalkboard, which she calls "a portal through the ages", bearing on it as the "address" the year of a specific historical event: 29th July, 1525. A series of props are placed on the table: a bowl of fruit, a silver papier mâché breastplate with matching helmet, a wooden sword, a feathered headband, a straw hat, an empty flower vase and a top hat. A classmate, along with an assistant, is asked to come forward. Choosing the breastplate and the helmet, the former writes the title of the specific historical event on the "portal": The Founding of Santa Marta. His assistant dons the feathered band and grabs the fruit bowl, and the two of them proceed to enact the scene in front of the class. The helmeted "time-traveller" then takes the wooden sword, clears his throat and places the weapon on the head of the kneeling fruit-offering "native" in a gesture of accolade before enunciating in a commanding tone:

"The year is 1525, and today 29th July is the date of the founding of the city of Santa Marta. I, Don Rodrigo de Bastidas, come in peace as envoy of the Spanish crown, hereby making known my intention to plan and build the first city in continental America, as well as to carry out the construction of a settlement, with proper roads and houses, for the benefit of the indigenous population."

The second demonstration, "The Colombian Declaration of Independence", is no less theatrical than the first and the roles are suitably performed by two other colleagues who, upon being summoned, both take to the front of the class with the gusto of seasoned thespians. Writing the title of their assigned historical event on the "portal", both proceed to "travel through time and space" to entertain and educate in equal measure. At the end of the lesson, all the performances are acclaimed by those in attendance with rapturous applause.

During the break we all sit around a mango tree, some of us with refreshments in hand purchased from the kiosk in the middle of the courtyard. Others peer over my shoulder as I continue to add and refine features to a face that refuses to leave my imagination. In the end, one of the girls decides that the long-haired female strikes her as familiar.

"That's so obviously Cinderella, look at the eyes."

"No, it isn't", says another. "That hair can only belong to Rapunzel."

"Seriously? Can't you tell it's the spitting image of Sleeping Beauty?"

While the girls continue to correct one another, some of the lads from class swoop from behind me, notebooks in hand, while I am still struggling with putting the finishing touches to the portrait.

"Miguel Ángel, did you bring your colouring pencils? Can you help us out with some maps we need for tomorrow's geography lesson?"

"Of course. Leave your books right here."

Knowing it is going to be a long day after a sleepless night, I lie back on the ground where we are sheltering from the midday sun and rest my head on my hands. While the notebooks are placed on my chest one by one, I catch the honeyed tones of light filtering through the canopy of leaves above and close my eyes thinking this might be as bad as life is ever likely to get. Except for the traumatic event of my first day at school, an event now relegated to some distant past, I rejoice in an everlasting present well-lived, solid bonds forged with classmates from infancy and abundant occasions of camaraderie and celebration punctuating our lives at regular intervals. I did not realise, however, that we had been inhabiting a perpetual state of joyful normality fostered by a beguiling sense of unending calm and protection.

CHAPTER 6

The Clock

Late November, 1976

From the moment he was spotted coming out of the F-2 headquarters that sunny afternoon in the company of his assigned group of agents, Sarmiento, alias 'El Totumo', smiled with anticipation. His tiny teeth were in full display whilst he rubbed his small hands with the same jubilant gesture of glee he employed every time he emerged victorious from the endless pinball machine sessions he was fond of inflicting on his work colleagues in assorted establishments of the northern perimeter of the city.

As usual, he wore a pair of dark glasses to protect his eyes from the sun, leaving behind him a trail of cologne that could be smelled from a long distance as he walked towards the vehicle that would be carrying him and his band of enforcers. Once on board, he caressed a chunky 24-karat gold crucifix set with a conspicuous emerald in the centre, to which he attributed his good luck.

It was not unusual for 'tasks' to be delegated to the group from time to time, and thanks to his unfailing gift of the gab, he had just secured the responsibility of arranging and coordinating yet another "lightning operation". These were crackdowns conducted by the police in the poorest communes that dotted the northern sector of the city, which invariably yielded the capture and detention of what the agents liked to refer to as "the usual suspects".

Even among his own colleagues, however, Sarmiento possessed the unenviable reputation of being the most slippery and cowardly member of this group of officers. In spite of his short stature, he seemed incapable of going about any of his businesses unnoticed. His predilection for drama, indiscretion and being the centre of attention had earned him the antipathy of his colleagues, amongst whom circulated the saying: the fastest way to spread a well-kept secret was to tell 'El Totumo'.

His penchant for hogging the limelight notwhitstanding, he was unfailingly the first to hide when trouble arrived and would vanish from sight when bullets started to fly during police operations. When it came to rumours, however, he boasted of possessing the most effective network of informants in Santa Marta, which he proudly called his 'antennas of the city'. While he never quite succeeded in gaining the trust of his superior, Sarmiento was reluctantly acknowledged for the reliability of his sources and always appeared to have useful last-minute information at his disposal.

For Sarmiento, however, nothing in this world afforded him more pleasure than the opportunity to play 'enemy number one of the underworld', subjecting his prey to humiliating methods of torture and watching undiluted panic forming in the eyes of his victims.

Whenever he could, the man who aspired to become Lieutenant Carrasco's right hand man was fond of giving free rein to his sadistic tendencies, fully enabled by his official credentials as an active member of the F-2.

La Castellana, the emblematic cradle of Colombian football, was a pitch built on a flat arid quadrant located in Pescaíto, a neighbourhood immortalised in local culture by dint of being the birthplace of Unión Magdalena, Santa Marta's football team, also known as the 'bananero cyclone', where generations of local heroes such as 'El Pibe' Valderrama first honed their skills before acquiring fame and recognition on the sporting world stage.

That fateful afternoon, the normally turfed venue was scarcely more than a dusty pitch awaiting resurfacing. On such occasions, local youths from the neighbourhood would be granted use of the facility, which was a mere stone's throw away from the mythical railroad that reached Santa Marta all the way from the Zona Banananera, finally reaching the sea port area by Punta Betín. Here, two teams of young players were engaged in a football match with a handful of spectators with buckets of water containing fizzy drinks to keep them cool.

At precisely four o'clock, a dark armoured vehicle with blacked-out windows made an unexpected incursion at full speed through the main gate of the venue, tires screeching in the sand and kicking up a blanket of dense yellow dust as it came to an abrupt stop in the middle of the pitch. Jorge, a 17-year-old boy and one of Diego Alberto Jesús Andrade's companions, was on the pitch along with others from his block when two armed men got out of the vehicle. Addressing those who had used the curtain of dust as camouflage to flee, Sarmiento announced in a loud raucous voice: "Where do you think you're all going? Nothing is happening. Those who are still here just stay exactly where you are. The others who decided to make a run for it will have to answer later. We know where you all live!"

Standing in the middle of the pitch in full view of petrified observers, he smiled and asked: "It's boiling in here! Are none of you going to treat me and my colleagues to a bottle of soda?"

An unpleasant surprise awaited the boys who had made for the exit. They had barely made it outside the venue when half a dozen uniformed police officers who had been lying in wait tackled them to the floor, promptly immobilising them. Emerging from the pitch and without ceasing to smile, Sarmiento walked slowly and peculiarly in the over-rehearsed manner of a spaghetti-western cowboy, fully immersed in the moment as somebody who loved to give a performance while the light of the afternoon glinted off the metal rim of his designer sunglasses. He headed towards one of the boys being held against a wall by two uniformed police officers. In a booming voice and without turning his head, he addressed the other suspects now spread-eagled on the dusty ground: "If you all keep running away every time you see me... guess what! Everyone will think you've been up to no good!"

He stopped in front of the frightened boy and scrutinised him through his dark glasses, studying the mixture of sand and sweat dripping down the young man's face. The suspect was barefoot, his straight hair reddish from the intense sun. Most tellingly, he wore a blue T-shirt with a yellow crocodile stamped on one side of it, just as the young tourist had described.

Sarmiento broke into another reptilian smile that exposed a row of small and crowded teeth and grabbed the boy's cheek, forcing the young man even closer to him as though he could smell the boy's fear. Then whispered to his face in a mocking, recriminatory tone:

"Seriously? Don't you even know how to hide? Still wearing the same T-shirt. Or can't mum afford to buy you a new one?"

Shortly after, official radio bulletins began spreading the news that the authorities had dealt a significant blow to organised crime with the capture of a number of suspects in the northern region of the city, although as usual, precise details of the operation remained vague and minimal. For the people of the city, the scenario had a sense of déjà vu.

"Chess is a lot like life."

I am in the refuge of our school library during my lunch break, ensconced in the upper level of my school, like so many times before when I did not feel like joining my other classmates in another game of football in the dusty heat of the afternoon sun. I am sitting on the floor, listening intently as I look at the enormous wooden chess board, pondering on the shape and design of the battalion of pieces laid out in front of me. Sitting with legs crossed opposite and surrounded by bookcases bursting with tomes and encyclopedias, is Francesca, the eldest daughter of Tamara Escovedo, principal of our primary school.

"All life is based on strategy", she states with certainty and a flourish of her hands, enunciating each syllable with the studied rhythm and cadence of someone well versed at speaking in public. I keep hearing that word from her lips, unsure as to its meaning.

"A plan of action", Francesca qualifies immediately, as though she can read the puzzlement on my face. "No goal you set yourself is truly a goal if it doesn't have a plan of action. You will realise how essential a lesson this is when you grow up, whether you are choosing a career or apply for a job."

As fond of Francesca as I was, her words did sound too much like adult talk to my ears, resulting in a lot of tuning out on my part – even when she recited the various, imaginatively named moves through which an opponent could be vanquished, such as The Bishop's Endgame, The Thunderbolt, The Queen's Sacrifice and The Rook and Pawn Endgame, which she took particular joy in describing. In truth, I listened intently but was infinitely more fascinated with the geometry and symmetry of the game's black and white grid, stark in its simplicity, whilst remaining fascinated by the shapes and individual roles assigned to each of the different chess pieces, rather than in how chess grandmasters had made their names throughout history. Thinking about the advantages and limitations of each piece, I was both amused and bemused by the limited ability of the King to manoeuvre and fend for himself, as opposed to the more versatile Queen, who enjoyed more independence and was capable of a far wider range of movements. This was an accurate reflection of the world I was growing up in, accustomed as I was to being surrounded and supported by female role models, my mother being the most inspirational of all, someone who, like the Queen in chess, had shown herself to be fiercely independent and just as versatile. And the fact that all our teachers at school were women made me suspect that, whilst it may indeed be a man's world, there surely had to be a great number of women doing a fair bit of orchestration behind the scenes.

I carry this thought along with me all the way back home until the blue school bus drops me off. Manuela, our housekeeper, had already ensured that supper was ready. And, just like clockwork, as whenever mum was going to be late from work, the phone rings. I hear her telling me it is going to be another long day at the office but that she will definitely be home before too long. I look into our back yard through the kitchen window whilst drinking a glass of water and, as improbable as it seems, Georgiana is sitting there in splendid solitude, dressed in summer clothes and wearing a large straw hat to protect her skin from the sun, her ubiquitous English-Spanish dictionary by her side, surrounded by trees swaying in a gentle breeze and her lithe form illuminated by the last golden rays of the afternoon sun, as if she is the reason it is there at all.

By the time I emerge from the shower, change clothes and get my school books ready for the next day, it is already dark. A heated up supper awaits me at the table where mother and Georgiana are already engaged in another one of their animated, gesture-laden conversations.

"I live in a London neighbourhood called Belgravia", Georgiana is telling her. "As soon as I'm able to reorganise my life back home, I would so love you both to come over and visit me."

Later in the evening, our guest and I watch television on the sofa in the lounge area and sit through a gamut of North American programs dubbed in Mexico. It isn't until Georgiana decides to sing along to *Gilligan's Island* and *The Beverly Hillbillies* that I realise the theme tunes that were so familiar to me in Spanish had in fact been originally conceived in English.

My most abiding memory of Georgiana was the occasion when, frustrated by the language barrier, she ended up drawing in one of my notebooks what looked like a castle featuring a huge clock tower at one end. She then wrote the words 'Big Ben' above the clock in large letters before reading out the words to me and pointing to herself with her index finger.

Taking a closer look at the drawing, I asked, somewhat in disbelief: "You live in a clock?", before realising 'Big Ben' represented a real clock in a real location.

A popular television commercial at the time publicising Colman's mustard immediately sprang to mind. "There are three things in life that always stay the same: Big Ben, The Changing of the Guard, and Colman's", announced the voiceover, along with corresponding stock black-and-white images of the clock tower and soldiers on horseback wearing their famous bearskin hats.

Following this discovery, and seeing a chance to form some common ground with Georgiana, I developed the habit of turning on the television after getting back from school, in the hope that that commercial would be broadcast so that our stranded visitor could see it with her own eyes. One evening, after what seemed like an eternity sitting in front of the television, the commercial was finally shown and we both did a spontaneous little dance in front of the screen. She uttered the words 'my home', before turning to me with a lingering smile of joy that seemed to light up the room.

My introduction to a faraway land called England had just begun.

CHAPTER 7
Birds of Prey

A legend had gradually been forming around 'The Birds of Prey'. Throughout the early 1970s, Santa Marta was still an unassuming coastal resort barely on the national radar, a pleasant backwater to be enjoyed once or twice a year by tourists attracted by the beauty of its beaches and the breathtaking spectacle of its sunsets. Which is why commentators from other parts of the country found it remarkable that Jaime Bateman Cayón, a charismatic young intellectual from one of the city's less affluent neighbourhoods should enjoy levels of popularity undreamed of by most politicians. This local *cause célèbre* had achieved the rare feat of resonating with both cognoscenti and university students across the country despite being the visible face of and mastermind behind the subversive group M-19.

Against the backdrop of this phenomenon, not a single week would go by without local media reporting on the grisly discovery of bodies, either displaying a single shot through the head or with their throats slashed, the majority of the victims found semi-hidden in wasteland within the urban perimeter. There was a palpable sense that something out of the ordinary was going on. Rumours that a gang of vigilantes operating on the fringes of justice was responsible for the disappearance and murder of petty criminals was gaining more and more traction among the population. 'The Birds of Prey', a colourful term coined by the tabloids, had seeped into local folklore. This catchy moniker, alluding to what most citizens suspected was a secret cabal of executioners taking the law into their own hands, was whispered in hushed tones among the fraternity of the underworld and was even used by parents as a bogeyman with which to admonish and reprimand their disobedient children.

The average *samario* (person from Santa Marta) was an ancestral amalgam of creole and native Caribbean, easy going by nature and with a tendency to follow the path of least resistance. Characterised by a sense of *joie de vivre*, a love of football and an apparent ability to dismiss adversity by dancing life's troubles away, a residual fatalistic streak led him or her to believe that most of life's unsavoury outcomes were the inevitable consequences of questionable courses of action or just plain bad decision-making. Sociable and argumentative in equal measure, *samarios* enjoyed entertaining one another with stories and liked nothing more than unpicking mysteries during endless rounds of conversation and debate with like-minded company, preferably over the course of a few cold drinks.

Samarios were also very fond of theorising, perfecting it to an art form. If anyone was found dead in suspicious circumstances, the default explanation pointed to the deceased keeping the wrong company or that, one way or another, the unfortunate individual must have had it coming. This tendency for impulsiveness would then be tempered by episodes of reflection and soul-searching until, eventually, most came to the conclusion that any event, whether good or bad, was best attributed to the will of God. But an undercurrent of uneasiness born out by the mysterious daily disappearances of small-time young criminals and an attendant rising body count had made the community stop to consider the state of society as a whole. Many were increasingly arriving at the troubling conclusion that the city's finest were turning a blind eye to extrajudicial killings, perhaps even welcoming the intervention of ruthless vigilantes who to all intents and purposes appeared to be doing the job for them far more swiftly and efficiently.

Upon hearing reports that five unidentified bodies had been found on the same day and brought to the city morgue of San Miguel cemetery, roving radio reporter Ricardo Gonzaga decided to pay a visit there, taking his tape recorder with him. The morgue was famously in full view of commuters and passengers going along Avenida Santa Rita, one of the main arterial roads of the city. Before it was eventually bricked up, the *'anfiteatro'*, as it was known, was nothing more than a diminutive chamber with whitewashed brickwork and a single slab of concrete usually occupied by a dead body. This was the sight that greeted Gonzaga as he stood on the pedestrian pavement while waiting to be granted access to the morgue. Narciso Castro, the city's eccentric coroner, was always at hand to chat to reporters while still engaged in his grisly occupation, autopsy saw in one hand and an *empanada* in the other. A small group of passers-by had already gathered around the facility to survey the corpses lying on the grass by the time the sun had set on the horizon. The scene had been rendered even more macabre by a sudden electricity outage, which made it necessary for the forensic team to conduct the grim business of examining the bodies by candlelight.

31

"In addition to the body lying inside the morgue, I can see four more victims in front of me, all found on wasteland... now lying face up on a grassy patch by the side of the *anfiteatro* since there's no room for them inside the morgue. The light is now very poor, but I can tell our listeners that each one of the victims has had their throat slashed."

Like his fellow colleagues at Radio Galeón, who included the legendary Aurelio Carbonell Estrada, an unrelenting thorn in the side of Santa Marta's corrupt ruling class, Gonzaga was a seasoned reporter fully accustomed to covering tragic events with rigorous detachment. Today, however, his customary verbiage and eloquence had all but abandoned him and his voice cracked with emotion as he spoke into the tape recorder.

"They are all wearing sports clothing and no shoes. And none appear to be older than eighteen."

It was against this backdrop of growing urban tension that Carmen Monzón, a civil servant working for the army, was first offered the opportunity to transfer from the S-1 staff team in what was then known as the Córdova Infantry Battalion 5 of the Colombian National Army to the State Police Department. Recruitment in this area had become a priority for the Government of Magdalena and there was sudden demand for experienced work staff, preferably those with a military background. Following a Statutory Decree, and with superiors in the battalion attesting to her sense of responsibility and professional integrity, she was duly appointed within the organization known as the F-2, which back then was the foremost branch of the state police.

As part of her daily routine, she would arrive early in the morning, passing through familiar scenes of street vendors carrying food and other wares food in makeshift street trolleys, shouting at the top of their lungs. Having exchanged her regular greetings with some of the well-known characters of the street, including Forero, who could be seen shining shoes opposite the headquarters, she entered the building and headed straight for her office, where she proceeded to make brief morning phone calls to the school and to her home before finally sitting down at her desk. Unlocking a drawer in which she kept her personal file, she retrieved a copy of the statement of detention processed by herself on the day she interviewed Georgiana's assailant and began to read through the contents with a sense of déjà vu. Closing her eyes, she recalled events that had taken place in her first month in the job, starting with when Chief Lieutenant José Francisco Carrasco was seen pacing around the department like a caged panther.

Those in the workplace knew him to be an impatient and inscrutable man of few words. Perspiring profusely, the Lieutenant briefly disappeared inside his office before re-emerging to resume his brooding march around the precinct, the rotor blades of the electric ceiling fans the only sound to be heard.

Having repeated this bizarre ritual several times, Carrasco finally stopped in the middle of the hub where Carmen had been sharing office space with some colleagues. Glowering at her, her superior exclaimed in a voice that made the office enclosures shake: "Where the hell are the written statements from last Saturday?"

Perhaps it was the oppressive heat in the headquarters taking a toll on Carrasco's judgement, despite his having the only office with air conditioning in the entire building. Irrespective of his reasons for the display, it appeared the chief of staff had been unable to locate certain files that some member of staff had processed over the weekend. Calmly but clearly, Carmen reminded him in front of all present that, as her contract of employment had been stipulated by the Government of Magdalena, her work shift was confined to schedules from Monday to Friday and did not include working shifts on Saturdays or Sundays.

For a horrible moment, the lieutenant's eyes looked as if they might pop out of their sockets. He stared silently at Carmen for what felt to everyone like an never-ending minute. Then, drawing a giant breath of air, Carrasco turned on his heels and entered his office, slamming the door shut behind him. From that moment on, and as had been her policy while in the army, Carmen always took the precaution of keeping personal copies of any document that passed through her hands and carried her signature.

She emerged from her office and stopped by the courtyard doorway to get some air. But the air that filled her lungs was rancid, almost evil-smelling. It was then she noticed something shifting in the dark inside one of the detention cells at one end of the yard. She approached the area of detention with trepidation.

The cells of the F-2 headquarters were famously devoid of electricity, water supply or even a seating area. The prospect of spending a night secluded in one filled criminals with dread. It was said many preferred incarceration in the legendary Panóptico Municipal, a nineteenth-century jail nicknamed 'fourteen windows', from which nobody had ever escaped and which felt more like an asylum than a prison. The F-2 detention cells consisted of four concrete walls no bigger than a toilet cubicle, and lacking that facility. Any detainee who dared to urinate or defecate in them risked a severe beating by officers, which is why a ban on food or drinks was always enforced on newly apprehended suspects.

Once Carmen peered through the rusty metal bars and could make out the shape of a young girl curled up on the floor. She quickly surveyed the courtyard behind before making a furtive attempt to communicate with the detainee through the cell bars.

"Hello there... Are you feeling well? It's quite all right... I'm here if you need anything"

The girl turned her head slowly toward the light as though awakened from a deep slumber. She then spoke with a voice like sandpaper, creating an echo in the empty diminutive chamber.

"Please... can I have some water? I'm very thirsty".

Carmen promised her she would not be long and promptly returned with two cups of water from an indoor dispenser. The sentry, who had just taken his position at the opposite end of the patio, looked on pretending to be oblivious to the development. The girl gulped the contents of both cups one after the other in quick succession and then gasped for air. Carmen took a good look at the girl now standing before her. She was wearing tight denim trousers and a skimpy top, her hair gathered at the top of her head and hanging down the sides. Traces of red lipstick were smudged around her mouth and across her chin. For the first time, the girl lifted her bloodshot eyes to look at her benefactor.

"What's your name?", asked Carmen, as she retrieved the empty cups from the girl.

"Natalia. And I swear I haven't done anything wrong." She appeared to be uninjured but displayed clear signs of anxiety.

Carmen then tried to calm her down with some words of reassurance. "I believe you. You've been here for nearly 48 hours and cannot legally be held imprisoned for another night. I've seen this happen before plenty of times. They tend to get very forgetful about their detainees in this place, but I'll see that I stick around just in case. It's more than likely you will be reunited with your loved ones before too long."

Natalia Mendoza was 20 years of age and unfamiliar to Carmen. But she had observed enough macho dynamics in the department to know that girls such as Natalia were routinely on the receiving end of appalling abuse from the men the moment they were brought into custody. On occasions like this, Carmen usually made a point of staying at the office long after her shift had ended in order to assist the female detainees and above all to keep a watchful eye on the men's behaviour.

As a matter of routine, the F-2 would carry out weekly raids on the notorious Calle de Las Piedras, using licence review of local establishments as a pretext to make their incursions into the sector. These operations, arranged and conducted by a handful of enforcement officers availing themselves of impounded foreign vehicles, invariably yielded the detention of a number of local women who plied their trade as prostitutes in order to make a living, a situation unchanged since the tail end of the nineteenth century, when Santa Marta's northernmost commune became a popular haunt for Jamaican and European sailors seeking to join the workforce during the construction of the city's railway.

When Carmen returned to the headquarters carrying a small brown paper bag containing a couple of *empanadas* she had bought from a street vendor, she crossed paths in the corridor with two agents on their way back from the cells in the courtyard.

"There goes María Teresa of Calcutta", one of them muttered to his colleague as they walked past. Carmen could hardly conceal her anger but chose to ignore them, to avoid an altercation. She continued towards the yard without breaking her stride, until she reached the concrete cell holding the girl, its dark recesses damp and claustrophobic.

"I've brought you something to eat. These will keep you going. I have it on good authority you won't be spending another night in this place. And what's more, I'll see to it that you are released before the day is out."

"I've heard of you", the young woman confided while making the *empanadas* disappear one by one. "My friends tell me what a blessing it is to have someone like you watching over them when things get too rowdy around here..." Suddenly remembering her predicament, she stressed angrily, "I wasn't doing anything illegal nor was I resisting arrest when they swooped down on us out of nowhere like hawks. I just happened to be in the wrong place at the wrong time."

During a moment of reflection, the girl looked Carmen in the eye for the first time. "I know what I do is frowned upon. But I have a sister that requires constant medical treatment and two younger brothers that I'm trying to put through school".

"I am not here to condemn any of the choices you felt you had to make for yourself", replied Carmen, "I'm aware of how hopeless the situation must seem for many young women in your part of town."

Suddenly becoming aware of the sentry's prying eyes, she hesitated for a moment and wondered whether her observation could just as easily apply to women from all walks of life, and not necessarily to those who just happened to be from the so-called wrong side of the tracks.

"Doña, I am not going to forget all you have done for us in this hellhole."

For a long moment, the two women held hands through the metal bars in a silent gesture of solidarity as the bells of the cathedral began to toll in the distance and a late afternoon breeze blew through the dusty yard.

CHAPTER 8

The Instrument

For the best part of a decade, Lieutenant Carrasco had nurtured the conviction that his career transfer from his native Medellín to the city of Santa Marta as chief of police of the F-2 had been nothing more than the direct result of divine intervention. Following the dictates of a dogma he obstinately believed infallible, Santa Marta, that small and retrograde coastal town he considered to be mostly populated by lazy coast-dwellers who would turn to petty crime at the first opportunity, was the ideal setting for the enactment of his particular brand of justice, a justice he would administer swiftly and robustly and in accordance with an unflinching belief that he was a living instrument of the law sanctioned and abetted by the highest power in the land. Now that he was chief of police, he saw himself as having legitimate mandate to inflict his vision of social engineering on a population of approximately a quarter of a million inhabitants.

The neighbourhood known as Barrio Jardín, the place where the government had granted him accommodation fit for someone of his position, was a model of orderliness and cleanliness. It was among the most coveted and quietest in the city, a collection of colonial-revival houses arranged in uniform rows in an orderly grid system, where all the properties had private guards and household refuse was collected five days a week.

As usual after work, he parked his vehicle in his private garage, activating a powerful air-conditioning system by flicking a switch in a compartment of the room and, without turning on the light, walked up a set of stairs to his shelter within a shelter: a terrace-like watchtower at the summit of the property, a vantage point offering an uninterrupted view of the neighbourhood's immediate surroundings, a private space that Carrasco used as a sanctuary for his meditations and where he sat chain-smoking cigarettes in almost absolute tranquillity until the sun of a new day emerged from behind the neighbourhood's terracotta tiled roofs. The privacy afforded to him and his neighbours, a tightly knit bourgeoisie where no one seemed to meddle in anyone else's business, was the ideal environment for him to recharge his batteries and continue planning his next move.

Like any other police chief appointed by the state, he had received extensive military training. It was rumoured that he slept for no more than two hours at a time and always kept a loaded revolver under his pillow. The subordinates closest to him, who guardedly referred to him as "'Napoleon'" in allusion to their superior's tenacity and short physical stature, often heard him say that sleep was a complete waste of time.

For two weekends every month, he considered it his almost devotional duty to drive to Simón Bolívar airport, where his wife and two sons would arrive by plane all the way from Antioquia. Above all, Carrasco considered himself an exemplary family man. Despite the time-consuming intricacies of his profession, he never disregarded the importance of regular family activities, all of which he planned with precision and military rigor.

In addition to his personal vehicle, the garage of his house contained two beach motorcycles that his two teenage sons enjoyed riding to their heart's content, making incursions into the surrounding neighbourhoods and racing up and down the gridded streets of the southern parts of Santa Marta, carrying sufficient cash in their pockets to cover mechanical and fuel costs.

In the evenings, the itinerary included gastronomic outings in restaurants such as Panamerican, which guaranteed more discretion and privacy than other local establishments of note and where Carrasco also held periodic meetings with Gustavo Maldonado, acting governor of Santa Marta, opportunities that the chief of the F-2 would use to keep Maldonado informed of the latest seizures of marijuana shipments carried out by a select team of armed officers who, under Carrasco's command, undertook lightning crackdowns on recalcitrant drug traffickers who made the mistake of underestimating him.

This select team of government-sanctioned officers from various parts of the country included the notorious and enigmatic Valverde, who acted as Carrasco's right-hand man. Overall, the group enjoyed carte blanche to mete out a brand of "'border justice'", treating the city of Santa Marta as their own playground in the manner of the Far West while acting as unofficial executioners – something that was of paramount convenience for Carrasco because, above all, he detested getting his own hands dirty. And the errands he would routinely demand of his men were often messy and unpleasant affairs, which included the violent execution and disappearance of suspects and "'undesirables'", in harmonious alignment with his particular program of social cleansing.

According to Carrasco's deep-rooted beliefs, this backward Latin-Caribbean town was in dire need of an effective and sustained purge. Social cleansing was a drastic but necessary measure and the most effective means with which to impose his personal vision of public order, a vision he nurtured and implemented with the unerring conviction of a Pontifex Maximus.

To this end, like any skilled strategist, Carrasco ensured he kept key individuals such as Manuel Méndez Mantilla, the country's Director General of the Police, firmly on his side. The Lieutenant's influence extended as far as the seat of power of the Magdalena Governorate itself, whose top officials were more than willing to grant him whatever favour he requested, even if such petitions included the orchestration of irregular manoeuvres that strayed far from established legal parameters.

Meanwhile, the "'big fish'" of Samarian society, who were behind every major illegal narcotics operation in the country, breathed more easily with Carrasco at the helm of the F-2. After all, these were the same individuals that the Lieutenant counted among his most valuable allies, respected members of society's wealthiest and most influential clans, with whom he maintained a careful and symbiotic relationship that included spending leisure time together as families as well as partaking of religious activities every Sunday morning.

In his twisted reasoning, he figured the city's economy benefited greatly from land illegally appropriated by Santa Marta's increasingly prosperous oligarchy, wrenched from the calloused hands of humble cotton farmers in the Sierra Nevada to be used instead for the far more profitable cultivation of cannabis. This was an oligarchy which reaped colossal financial rewards from income generated by the export of "'the accursed weed'" to the United States, on the pretence that this newfound wealth would somehow trickle down society's strata, creating real opportunities for local employment and development – a fallacy of monumental proportions, given how rapidly the monetary bonanza was syphoned off by a handful of established families to finance an endless series of money-laundering operations while the authorities turned a blind eye.

The pleasant, easy-going folklore of the region, with the vibrancy of its tropical musical and the racial diversity of its mestizos and mulattoes, were as intolerable to Carrasco as the diabolical dry heat of the city that consigned him to hellish torment on a daily basis, often taking him to the brink of apoplexy. There was, however, an upshot to this occupational hazard which amply compensated for all the thorns in his flesh: unlike most men, Carrasco possessed the power, influence and the necessary tools to fulfil every single one of his ambitions under the guise of the law and as the city's protector-in-chief. After all, who would be foolish enough to keep an eye on the protectors?

Sunday mornings were exclusively devoted to church activities. As believers and parishioners, his family and associates all partook regularly of the liturgical emblems of the Holy Communion in Santa Marta's colonial basilica, where the remains of the Libertador Simón Bolívar were first laid to rest. Every Sunday of Mass was another opportunity for Carrasco to wipe the slate clean and attenuate the reproachful cries of his increasingly desensitised conscience.

In the midst of plumes of perfumed incense that pervaded every inch of the three naves of the cathedral, the priest's words reverberated across the cavernous structure as the concluding parts of his sermon were pronounced in portentous tones:

"Let everyone willingly submit to the higher authorities, for there is no authority on earth that does not come from God. The existing authorities have all been placed by God Himself in their relative positions. Therefore, anyone who opposes said authority has turned against the order established by God, and those who do so will bring judgment upon themselves."

One by one, man, woman and child, obediently stood in line as they waited to receive the holy sacrament of the Eucharist from the priest's hand to the tremulous sound of the old organ accompanying the Gregorian chant that now resonated throughout every corner and crevice of the colossal Renaissance cathedral.

"'Come now,' says the Lord, 'and let us reason together: though your sins be as scarlet, they shall be as white as snow; though they be red like crimson, they shall be as wool.'"

Hearing the words as they emanated from the priest's mouth, Carrasco felt pure and absolved, as if he had been born again.

CHAPTER 9

The Islet

Late November, 1976

One morning at school, our headmistress made an announcement before class which got the students talking excitedly amongst themselves.

"As you may remember, an annual regional drawing contest was instituted by the municipality to mark the 450th anniversary of the founding of the city of Santa Marta. One year on, we are delighted to announce this was not a one-off event. Pupils from all primary educational establishments in the region are again being encouraged to take part. As before, the idea is for participants to use their inspiration to produce an individual illustration based on anything of interest that catches your eye in the environment of Plaza Bolívar. Three works of art from three different pupils will be chosen by the judges. Corresponding prizes will also be awarded. We wish the very best of luck to any students here willing to represent our school".

The day of the contest was suddenly upon us, and pupils from all corners of the Magdalena region that had registered for the event appeared to be gathered in Plaza Bolivar, a public space offering splendid views of the bay as well as municipal buildings. However, no amount of mental preparation could pacify a very familiar sensation of butterflies in my belly.

I recall feeling the fresh sea breeze on my face as I walked alongside Francesca Escovedo, the school headmistress's eldest daughter and my sometime tutor. In addition to introducing me to the intricacies of board games during lunch hours without making any of it appear too intimidating, Francesca often acted as substitute teacher for history and geography lessons at my school. Full of excitement and armed with a roll of white card and a plastic pouch of coloured pencils that she was carrying for me in her artisan daybag, we made our way to the contest's designated open venue, illuminated as it was by a sizzling sun that was partially blocked by the Banco De La República building, a towering concrete monolith that looked out of place amongst the renovated colonial buildings overlooking the square. As we approached in the hope of securing a spot, it felt like entering a gladiatorial arena.

The buses that had transported us from our various schools were stationed in the periphery, including a minibus from the Divino Niño and another from a school called Montessori, the latter having the distinction of being the oldest of its kind in the country. The normally sedate square had been transformed into a hive of activity. Instructed by their respective tutors, a number of contestants were already hard at work or had already found their source of inspiration. I observed a fresh pineapple being precariously placed on one of the park's granite benches for a budding artist to copy. Another pupil attempted to capture the disparate proportions of assorted tropical fruit tastefully arranged on a pewter tray. Pupils from a different group were deep in concentration drawing the Four Faces caryatids sculpted from Italian marble, a decorative feature of the square's octagonal fountain erected in the nineteenth century to commemorate the abolition of slavery. Others could be seen skilfully producing sketches of street paraphernalia that coffee vendors had parked around the fountain. An equestrian bronze statue of Simón Bolívar taking place of prominence in the middle of the square, and whose horse standing on its hind legs appeared to defy the laws of gravity, had been completely surrounded by students attempting to capture its likeness. Francesca and I had been wandering from one place to another in search of a spot in which to get started, beneath the rays of an implacable morning sun, when I was suddenly brought low by an asthma attack. We decided to occupy seats in what seemed to be the only vacant granite bench in the square. From that vantage point, El Morro, an islet in the middle of the ocean, could clearly be seen through palm leaves that barely moved in the light breeze.

"I don't feel like taking part," I said with resignation as I put down my inhaler and looked at the large number of students around me. "It's going to be impossible for me to concentrate on very much at all today."

"Your competing in this was never meant to be an imposition," Francesca replied in an effort to ease my despondency. She wore her customary dark glasses, a hat to protect her short hair from the ravages of the sun and sober linen clothing that made her resemble an explorer of the Nile. "If you like, we can just sit here in the great outdoors soaking up the sun and people-watch until the competition time is up."

Feeling tense and without any energy, I rested my head on her lap and she placed her felt hat on my face to shield it from the sun. I crossed my arms across my chest like an embalmed pharaoh.

With her knack for storytelling, Francesca then began rolling back the centuries with tales of maritime derring-do by swashbucklers and buccaneers in order to keep me distracted. As usual, her romanticised description of what a Caribbean scenario must have been like four hundred years ago eventually gave way to striking historical anecdotes.

"Did you know that El Morro just ahead of us was used as a fortress during the Spanish occupation to safeguard the city against attacks by invaders and pirates?" she asked as though she was addressing a classroom.

"Didn't you once say many of those pirates were Englishmen?", I asked.

"At least according to the Spaniards, who held Sir Francis Drake to be amongst the most villainous Sea Dogs to sail the Atlantic. Pirates did much to alter the course of history across the Caribbean, changing the economy of the region and in Europe by targeting treasure ships sailing back to Spain and making off with all their gold and silver."

Francesca then turned her eyes in the direction of the sea port and mused. "They say behind every significant historic event there's always an Englishman."

I closed my eyes and visualised a vast expanse of sea swarming with buccaneer ships navigating around El Morro.

"That rock has been the city's first line of defence for four hundred years. One day you and I will sail there so you can see some of the cannons that are still left on the islet."

I removed her hat from my face and stared at the unblemished blue Caribbean skies above, the same skies that, six years after Columbus's discovery of the 'New World', must have witnessed the arrival of the first Spanish galleons captained by Don Juan de Ojeda, the fifteenth-century explorer and founder of El Ancón, the city's first settlement, situated just over a hundred yards north of the square.

I then directed my eyes towards the colossal rock in the middle of the sea that had been Santa Marta's immutable sentinel for hundreds of years. At its summit was a tall lighthouse illuminating the passage of all manner of vessels from all corners of the world, including the luxurious steamers of the United Fruit Company's Great White Fleet as they approached the city all the way from New Orleans, Havana, Panama, Cartagena de Indias and Puerto Colombia. I was staring entranced by the blue strip of water below the horizon when, seemingly out of nowhere, a gigantic white vessel cut across my field of vision, silently navigating towards the seaport at the far right of the bay.

I jumped up at once from my reclining position, anticipating that in less than a minute El Morro would be completely eclipsed by the enormous passing ship.

"Get up! There's no time to lose!", I exclaimed before running the few yards that separated us from the promenade, carrying along with me the backpack containing my drawing utensils.

"If you exit the designated area of the contest, they will disqualify you!", shouted my tutor adjusting her hat on her head with one hand while embarking in pursuit behind me.

Without losing sight of the ship's trajectory, I stopped right by the edge of the square, looking for a flat surface to unroll the piece of white card I had been carrying. Realising what I was trying to do, Francesca positioned herself in front of me, allowing me to unfurl the paper on her shoulders, which she then kept extended at the edges while keeping as still as possible, despite both of us still catching our breath.

I looked up again in the direction of the sea and there she was, majestic and resplendent in white, a moment forever encased in amber in the recesses of my memory. The islet was now completely concealed by the enormous cruise ship taking centre stage in the vast expanse of water. Guided by instinct, I delineated the contour of the gigantic mechanical wonder suspended as though in a time warp in the middle of the ocean. While doing my best to keep a steady hand as I busied myself with depicting straight rows of tiny windows visible above the vessel's hull, I asked Francesca what country was represented by the flag on the ship.

"Greece", responded Francesca from beneath. "The liner must have navigated the length of the Mediterranean and sailed here all the way across the Atlantic".

Greece. That remote country of intriguing and yet familiar-sounding names, I thought to myself, as I frantically continued to depict the fleeting scene before my eyes. Having spent late afternoons intently listening to students from Liceo Celedón discussing European history on the corner of grandmother's house, I found it fascinating that, despite being born and bred *samarios*, a good number of them, such as Euclides, Teófilo and Diógenes - who were just three of my classmates - had been given ancient Greek names by their parents. This persisting practice showed just how much of an indelible mark ancient Greek culture had left on western civilisation, including our so-called 'new world' of the Americas.

"Incidentally, every time you press down the point of that pencil on the card, it tickles…" giggled Francesca as I struggled not to lose concentration.

"And you… don't you spoil my lines with the juddering of your laughter…" I replied without taking my eyes off the cardboard.

The sound of bells began to reverberate throughout the square, announcing that the time allocated to the contest was coming to an end. Spotting a now empty public bench in the square, I ran towards it immediately. Realising I had mere minutes to spare, I included the islet in the composition and quickly rendered the Caribbean Sea around the ship by forcibly pressing down a blue crayon on the card, using the texture of the granite from the bench to create the effect of a choppy sea, until my right wrist felt like it was on fire. Members of the organising team were now swarming like bees around the square collecting pieces of artwork from participants and it wasn't long before one of them approached me from behind and unceremoniously removed the drawing from my sight. I remember feeling distraught in the belief that my drawing, as far as my self-critical eye was concerned, resembled little more than a haphazard collage of incoherent images in disparate rendering styles, all concocted under extreme duress.

Several days later, I found myself in attendance for the prizes announcement ceremony, along with dozens of other participants and school tutors, in a large municipal venue in the centre of the city. When the judges unexpectedly decided to select my piece as the winner of the contest and made me pose before local press photographers, I was completely gobsmacked.

The following day, a certain black-and-white photo in which I appeared, trophy in hand, tiny and sporting a nervous smile, was published on the front page of the local newspaper *El Informador*.

Little did I know that the publication of that picture would throw the course of my life into complete disarray.

CHAPTER 10

The Farewell

Late November, 1976

The days that followed were pervaded by a welcome sense of calm and normality in our house from the transformative presence of the tourist girl, with her otherworldly appearance and unusual tone of voice.

Our house was far from luxurious, quite unlike the whitewashed neo-colonial villas spread around the more privileged neighbourhoods west of town, but, looking back, it was a welcoming and comfortable place to be. It consisted of a spacious living room with plenty of light, a central dining room, three bedrooms, and a kitchen that led to a patio with a variety of tropical fruit trees planted all around, as well as access to a garage. There was also an L-shaped front garden and a small terrace by the front door. Our neighbourhood was relatively quiet and many of its streets had yet to be surfaced by the municipality.

I would spend hours ensconced in the privacy of my room putting the finishing touches to my drawing of our tourist. When I emerged, I would often find my mum and Georgiana playing cards in the sitting room like best of friends as the afternoon wore on.

"How can you waste your time playing games whose outcome depend on random luck?" I asked the pair bemusedly. "There are other games. Real games. Ones that allow for planning and … strategy".

"Now, there's a big word", replied mum, raising her eyebrows.

Georgiana sat there in silence, looking in my direction with what looked like a knowing smile. Following that episode, mostly because of the attention she was getting from my mother, I felt jubilant that I never caught the pair of them playing cards at the table again. As for my routine habits in the house, which included skipping tiles in our front room, a kind of therapeutic game to unwind after a day at school, inevitably conducted under Georgiana's curious eye, I couldn't help but feeling distracted by the novelty of being watched by a complete stranger, no matter how alluring.

As time passed, not only did she start to join me in my skipping-floor-tiles game after school, but she also indulged my newfound enthusiasm for role-playing learning tasks, such as the ones I had learned in history class. As a one-time nursery teacher, she appeared genuinely excited that innovative teaching methodologies to encourage students to deepen their understanding of history were being employed as educational tools in our primary schools.

During the following weeks, whenever mum's workload allowed, the two women would venture out to the city centre by car for some retail therapy or make periodic trips to the bank and the telegraph office. Georgiana loved her summer clothes and had taken to wearing colourful Santa Marta T-shirts decorated with painted horizons that mum would give her as presents, letting her choose them from the racks in department stores. Increasingly, it felt as if the girl from the other side of the world had eased into her new surroundings. She had gone from me cautiously referring to her in private as La Dama (literally, 'the lady', which in Spanish doesn't carry the same nobility-title connotations as it does in English), as well as 'she-of-the-hyphenated-surname', until I finally became sufficiently at ease to address her by her first name. As for her, she had progressed from calling me 'Michelangelo' to the much harder to pronounce Miguel Ángel. Eventually, I became comfortable with her presence in the house and, as far as both mum and I were concerned, she had seamlessly morphed into being an integral part of our family

On week days after class, I would run through the front of our house from the school bus, and just like clockwork she would be there in our back yard, practising an activity she called "meditation", before moving on to the kitchen to assist our housekeeper with the dishwashing or to indulge her newfound culinary abilities, such as making *arepas con queso*, a traditional recipe she had picked up from my mum.

Watching one of her yoga sessions, during which she seemed to defy the laws of physics by keeping perfectly still whilst standing on her head, I sensed I may have found a kindred spirit in Georgiana. With butterflies in my stomach, I finally felt brave enough to open up, in a bid to get to the bottom of the enigmatic tourist, despite the obvious language barrier, which appeared to be diminishing anyway with each passing day.

"Do you think you and I can get these, em, portals… to do something really useful?…" I cautiously asked whilst drawing a chalk line on the patio wall in the shape of an arch above my head, "so that, instead of travelling through time like we do in our history lessons, you and I could instead travel to and get a sense of where you actually come from?"

"I think we can do both!", she replied in that melodic voice of hers, eyes open wide. Smiling as though she was about to pull a rabbit out of an imaginary hat, she added: "Just watch!"

Grabbing a piece of coloured chalk from my pouch of utensils she produced an effortless arch across the wall with a single flourish. She knelt down, rendering in the middle an almost exact replica of the drawing she had made for me, the pointy tower she once again referred to as 'Big Ben', with a more elaborate clock face complete with Roman numerals, drawing clock hands that had fast forwarded us five hours into the future, effectively introducing me to the hitherto unknown concept of time zones and meridians. Turning to me, she stretched her arms open wide and announced: "Greenwich Mean Time!"

I confess to just standing there open-mouthed in amazement at what she had conjured up out of thin air. My brain grappled with the excitement of another fascinating discovery.

"I look forward to the day you and Carmen come to visit me in London, I will then take you to Greenwich", she smiled radiantly, "so you can see the real thing with your own eyes."

"Follow me!", I said to her, "there's something I want to show you just around the corner".

At one end of the patio, there was a hall area where the floor surface was covered in tiles which, if one squinted hard enough and used a bit of imagination, resembled a gigantic chessboard.

"This is where I have been playing a brand new game by myself. And here, from one end of this board to the other, is how you can help me get to your... Greenwich Meridian!"

"I'll see what I can do for you!", she played along without missing a beat, before asking quizzically: "Are there any rules in this game?"

"Absolutely! It works much like a game of chess, only I've narrowed it down using just a single piece to advance across the board."

Bringing back the mustard advert we had seen on TV featuring the Changing of the Guard, with soldiers on horseback resplendent in their polished metal chest plates, I requested uninhibitedly: "And you are going to help me get from Santa Marta to London by... horse – whose movement is like the shape of the letter "L"!" – "Which we both know stands for 'London', right? Okay. By horse it is!"

Fully engaging with the enactment, she pointed out: "In yoga we call it sending positive vibes. Your starting point, Santa Marta, is over here on this

48

side and, waiting for you across the board will be London – your final destination!"

Pleased with how she was able to finish my sentences and safe in the knowledge I was in good hands, I followed her directions to the letter. Using the horse's four-square forward movement and taking care not to miss a single step, I effectively reached the other side of the 'board' in my first attempt.

"You've done it, Miguel Ángel!", she exclaimed enthusiastically. "This means you are definitely coming to London!"

The musical intonation of her voice and the effortless elegance of her movements, akin to those of a ballet dancer, had become as commonplace as the birds singing in the orchards. While my previous perception of foreigners had been limited to watching them on TV shows, Georgiana now appeared as familiar and as natural as the summer breeze or the glow of the afternoon. In the course of our increasingly frequent interactions, I had come to discover a hitherto unknown vivacious side to her personality, at times coupled with a mischievous sense of humour. In a short space of time, her daily presence in our house represented a welcome break from the monotony of life.

One late afternoon, strains of salsa music could be heard from a radio in the neighbourhood as the three of us gathered in the lounge. I instinctively asked Georgiana if she wanted to dance, and for the first time I saw her cheeks turn bright pink.

"I can't dance to save my life!", she said.

"Nonsense. It's far easier than you think", I retorted, and proceeded to take both her hands in the middle of the sitting room while mum watched in delight.

"That's what the child says!", mum interjected, shrugging her shoulders.

"Take one step forward with your left leg, transfer your weight and then step back onto your right and collect – those are the basic steps – and just let the rhythm take over", I instructed with authority, before realising I was barely taller than her midriff.

"I have two left feet", she confided in a mortified tone.

"You're doing really well!" I countered, praising her gift for improvisation.

When the strains of music outside suddenly subsided, she chortled: "Saved by the bell!".

One Sunday morning, mum and I awoke to find Georgiana making breakfast in the kitchen, wearing Manuela's apron over one of her colourful

Santa Marta T-shirts. She arrived at the table with a large tray containing *arepas con queso*, along with scrambled eggs with chopped tomatoes and onions, a typical regional dish known as *perico*, as well as freshly made Colombian coffee. Her command of the Spanish language had grown exponentially, to the point where she had ceased to consult her English-Spanish dictionary and had even stopped mixing English expressions with her Spanish, which we had always found endearing. She still spoke to us in a voice that always made me think she was about to burst into song.

"As usual, I'm struggling to find the right words ... but I'd just like to say how grateful I am to you both for welcoming me into your house and making me feel like part of a family so far away from home."

Being the natural born storyteller she was, she brought to life intrepid adventures from around the globe, including her recent trek across the Andes to the city of Machu Picchu, and regaled us with tales of Kathmandu and Indonesia, exotic locations every bit as fascinating as the mythical idea of a green and pleasant land called England.

"Mum, can we take Georgiana on a trip to the farm so she can drink milk from the cows and feed the chickens? I want to see her in one of my bubbles!"

Looking puzzled for a moment, Georgiana reassuringly decoded that I wished to continue collecting memories of her presence in surroundings other than our house while she was still in our midst.

"The first thing I'm going to do when I get back to London is write to you. And I promise you both that my home will be your home. Whenever you feel ready to make the trip across the pond – and I appreciate it is a big pond – I'll be at the airport ready to greet you with open arms."

Early December, 1976

The last happy memory I have of Georgiana in our house was the occasion she helped us put up the Christmas tree one late evening during one of the sector's frequent electricity blackouts. For safety's sake, I had only been allowed to unpack the box containing the multi-coloured glass baubles while I watched the proceedings sitting in the lotus position I had learned from our yoga-practicing friend. By the time the electricity had come back on, the plastic conifer had been artfully covered in tinsel and all its decorations. As the pièce de résistance, Georgiana then reached inside the box and took the silver star made of cardboard and glitter. Standing on tiptoes, and breaking into the biggest smile I had seen on her face, she carefully placed the star at the top of the tall plastic tree while mum and I applauded in unison.

Early February, 1977

One night dominated by a clear sky and a full moon, and while the two women engaged in relaxed conversation on twin rocking chairs by the main entrance to our house, as had become customary for them before going to bed, the stillness and tranquillity of our street was interrupted by an approaching glow of lights and a crunching sound of tires on gravel. It became noticeably louder, until a procession of three dark Land Rovers, which mum immediately recognized as belonging to the F-2 patrol, came to a gradual stop outside our house.

The engines and lights were switched off one by one and for a few seconds all was silent until a group of men emerged from each vehicle. Spearheaded by agent Valverde, the men included Sarmiento and Vergara, all clearly visible under the street corner light, alongside cohorts Montoya and Cristancho, who were the last to exit the cars. Two other individuals remained inside one of the vehicles and their silhouette could be distinguished from the terrace.

The group of men carrying automatic weapons strapped to their shoulders engaged in idle chit chat and lit cigarettes on the corner of the pavement. Breaking away from the group, Valverde slowly approached the gate to our house. Greeting the two women, the agent crossed the threshold that led to the terrace. With a sense of déja vu, mum suddenly felt Georgiana's hand firmly gripping her wrist as the man stood before them. Forcing a smile, Valverde announced he had been given instructions by the lieutenant to collect Georgiana from the premises and escort her to the airport.

"What's with the show of force outside my house? Is there a good reason why you lot have turned up here unannounced and armed to the teeth?", mum enquired while Georgiana continued to grip her wrist in petrified silence.

Making an effort to appear amiable, Valverde glanced at Georgiana out of the corner of his eye: "Tell 'la 'gringa' not to worry. The team and I are having to take care of a few things later tonight."

He looked over at his armed colleagues, whose heads and shoulders were visible above the hedge that delineated the front garden, and went on. "Word has reached us that a smuggling boat owned by Otoniel Loaiza (a notorious trafficker) will be picking up merchandise by the coast around midnight. After we drop off the *gringa* at the airport, we'll be on our way to intercept that cargo, and we can't go unarmed."

"You say you are here to escort the girl to the airport? Have her documents been duly processed by the embassy?" my mother asked.

"Funny you should mention that. DAS processed her travel document through the embassy in Bogotá earlier today. And here's a warrant from the chief."

The agent thrust the papers into Carmen's face. "And while you're at it, feel free to check her itinerary."

Reaching inside his shirt pocket, Valverde produced a plane ticket. Carmen closely scrutinised both the warrant and the flight schedule, which included leaving the country on a plane departing in a few hours from Barranquilla to London via Miami.

To Carmen, the explanation seemed reasonable enough and the evidence of an official warrant was reassuring. Still, something about the way the men were behaving remained disconcerting.

Valverde offered: "I appreciate how all this looks to you, but the boys are just a bit restless. You know just as much as I how quickly things can unfold. Suddenly, we have an operation on our hands. In the meantime, we'd like to get on with taking the girl to the airport first, and then hope it's not going to be another one of those long nights."

Carmen could not help but notice the habitually grim Valverde being unusually talkative, as though he was eager to make the right impression.

"Stay right where you are, while we go inside for a moment. As you can see, the girl is confused and frightened. I need to break all this down to her."

Once inside the house, Georgiana began to tremble, unleashing tears of anxiety and despair. Hoping to reassure her with some choice words of encouragement in her limited English, mother held her in a prolonged embrace until she stopped sobbing.

Then, making a conscious effort to compose herself, Georgiana looked mum in the eye. "Please forgive my display. I didn't mean to cause a scene. I don't know what came over me."

"You are perfectly entitled to express how you feel in unusual circumstances such as these! No need to apologise at all!"

"I understood everything the agent just told you. I realise the time has come for me to go back home. My family must be worried sick about me and in some way the news from the embassy comes as a huge relief. I'm just not accustomed to seeing people brandishing guns!"

"Boys with their toys", added Carmen, "like they need to compensate for whatever it is that is missing from their lives, I suppose".

This last observation raised a barely restrained chuckle from them both. Wiping a tear from her face, Georgiana then smiled regretfully: "Tell Miguel Ángel I'm sorry I couldn't say goodbye to him."

"He hates farewells of any kind. In his own way he's been preparing for this day. He knew you had to go sooner or later. I can tell he's become really attached to you."

"The trouble is, I myself have become quite attached to you both. I'm going to miss you very, very much."

As for me, I had been far from asleep throughout all this, having been woken by the strange lights outside my window. For a while, I stood motionless and silent, spying through a gap in the curtains on the unusual scenes of dark vehicles and fleeting visions of barrels of guns glistening in the amber light.

Meanwhile, the women busily gathered the few belongings Georgiana had in her room. Moments later, both emerged from the house under the watchful eye of Valverde, who silently escorted the girl to the vehicle while another one of the men helped put her luggage in the back of the car.

Before getting into the vehicle, Georgiana turned to mum to remind her: "Don't forget you have a house in London. Come and visit me soon. I'll write as soon as I get home."

As the engines started, Georgiana made eye contact with mum one last time before one of the agents closed the door and she was barely visible through the tinted window.

Forcing another smile, Valverde addressed mum: "See you at the office tomorrow", before slipping into the back of the leading Ford Bronco.

The cars departed as cautiously as they had arrived, while mum stood watching from the terrace till the procession of vehicles had disappeared into the night.

The next few days unfolded without further incident. However, Georgiana's abrupt departure from the family environment of our house ultimately proved difficult for us to digest, and every day since her departure felt like a multitude of colourless days even when the sun was shining.

Meanwhile, my school routine continued pretty much as before, even if plans for me to stay at my grandmother's house remained unaltered. I was so accustomed to abiding by my mum's decisions that I had no objection to the arrangement, particularly when I knew I was going to have grandmother's extensive back yard all to myself, free to classify all manner of insects and animals in my notebook to my heart's content. I was more than eager to resume contact with the flora and fauna of that spacious place and looking forward to running and jumping among the fruit trees to the sound of birdsong. After arriving at the ancient great yellow mud brick house with its high walls and timbered zinc roof, I watched grandmother unpacking the bags that contained my school uniform and assorted other items before neatly organising everything inside a wooden cupboard reeking of mothballs.

The days after Georgiana's departure were punctuated by a dramatic increase in activity at the F-2 headquarters. Amidst a glacial atmosphere of awkward silence and guarded looks from Carmen's colleagues in law enforcement, the sight of large trolleys with precariously balanced containers brimming with drugs and contraband being pushed noisily down the main corridor to a warehouse space used by operations personnel as repository for confiscated merchandise had become a regular feature outside her office. By the end of the first week, the warehouse had been filled to capacity and every corner of the dependency reeked of the pungent smell of cannabis. Disconcertingly, and despite all the activity and reports in the local press advertising what a significant blow to the criminal underworld these series of operations had been, Carmen wondered why there had been no sign of any captured smugglers. Most peculiarly, the absence of police records in the official archives corroborating the success of any particular operation prompted Carmen to become even more meticulous in keeping track of irregularities than ever before. Consequently, the personal archive of copies that she continued to keep safely in her desk grew exponentially with each passing week.

More chilling for her was having to walk past the now vacant space in the street where Forero, the discapacitated shoeshiner, had used to set up the utensils of his trade. The portion of pavement occupied by this most familiar of faces, whose unexplained absence had become a matter of conjecture amongst the locals, was an almost insignificant patch a short distance across the street from the F-2 headquarters. As the days wore on, the vacuum of solitude and emptiness of that square metre of space appeared to glare at Carmen on her daily commute to work with an increasingly haunting intensity.

The days passed, turning into weeks, and Georgiana's written communication from London failed to materialise. Despite appearing to have covered every conceivable subject under the sun with her in their frequent conversations, from adventures in the Far East, photography, horses, fashion, university life and scuba diving, Carmen regretted not having pressed her for details of her home address or even a contact number. Georgiana's assurances of welcoming us to London in a not too distant future had doubtlessly been heartfelt and genuine. In retrospect, however, she never chose to divulge information of a fixed abode, not even on a scrap of paper. Even so, it remained Carmen's vehement wish that the girl who had left such a hole in our lives had safely settled back in her homeland. She attributed the delay of the promised correspondence to the everyday vicissitudes of life, assuming that mail would always be slow crossing the Atlantic.

Late April, 1977

Meanwhile, back at the F-2 headquarters, the recurring resurgence of a decade-long vendetta between the Cárdenas and Valdeblánquez clans, two notorious families from La Guajira, had seen a significant increase in violent deaths in the city, with the resulting fast-tracking of witnesses and suspects at the police department hub. That afternoon, in a bid to avoid what the Lieutenant referred to as 'undesirable backlogs', Carmen was asked to take over duties at the fingerprinting department, where she spent the remainder of the day processing reports of two suspects that had been brought into custody that day, along with statements from an assortment of witnesses from the general public. In addition, she had been instructed to act as courier to relay newly compiled documentation to the relevant courts for the possible conviction of a number of detainees.

The routine office work had taken the best part of the afternoon but Carmen never knowingly refused any request to help speed up the processing of paperwork at the hub. Despite a certain antipathy that had been brewing against her over the months, one thing officials could agree on was that the female ex-army official was both dependable and efficient at her job.

Having taken a seemingly endless multitude of fingerprints and completed all relevant reports with the trusty Olivetti typewriter that had served her so well since her days in the battalion, she briefly stopped to clear her head. She noticed the traces of black dactyloscopy ink smeared on her fingers and palm of her right hand, so, carefully placing the official papers in a folder and taking care not to stain any pages with ink, she headed to the ladies' room to wash her hands.

The black ink proved difficult to remove under the running tap. Carmen stood silently by the sink for some time to process her thoughts and, for a few minutes, the faint sound of running water was the only sound that could be heard.

It was during that brief space of time that she was alerted by approaching steps from two individuals who then entered the adjacent men's room. Once inside, the men started a conversation which could be heard through the partition wall between. A faint smell of stale beer even reached Carmen's nostrils. One of the voices belonged to Agent Vergara, alias 'Espuela', who was in charge of the motor section department. The dependency was generally a noisy environment, but at that particular location close to the Lieutenant's office, there was relative stillness.

The conversation that followed chilled Carmen's bone to the marrow:

"You had an obsession with that *gringa*..."

"Oh, come on, we all had a thing about her..."

"Valverde... the guy's a right sadist..."

"Yeah... what he did was... God Almighty, even when you know what a nasty piece of work he is... it's still quite shocking what he's capable of..."

"I still can't get over that business in Los Alcatraces..."

"Listen... be very careful around Carmen, she always looks like she knows something... good thing the boss is getting really pissed at her and her attitude..."

The lurid exchange continued for a few more seconds until Carmen finally heard the men's disembodied voices and steps gradually echoing away down the outside corridor until they had vanished.

Somehow, Carmen had managed to turn off the running tap and had silently locked herself in one of the bathroom's two small cubicles, prostrating herself on her knees in front of the toilet basin and making an effort to ensure her accelerated breathing remained as discreet and as silent as possible.

Overcome by spiralling tension and anxiety, an icy sweat began to roll down her temples and her extremities had become tense and rigid. Her idealistic concept of the Colombian mechanism of justice which she had held sacrosanct from a very early age had collapsed in a matter of seconds.

She felt like vomiting, but felt unable to satisfy that biological need without risking attracting attention to herself. Silently, she prayed nobody would enter the room while she wrestled alone with her emotions in that rectangular, claustrophobic space.

Every fibre of her being screamed for self-preservation and running away the moment she believed it would be safe to do so. And yet, prompted by her conscience and a primal, unassailable belief in human dignity, she knew she had no choice but to confront her superior as soon as possible.

Composing herself, she finally stood up and left the bathroom, walking decisively towards Carrasco's office. Without knocking on the door, she burst into her superior's office, surprising the lieutenant sitting at his desk on his own.

In a stern, firm voice, she made her demand known in no uncertain terms: "I'd like you to tell me what is happening."

Rapidly concealing his initial shock, Carrasco replied with a mixture of disdain and disbelief: "Carmen, what the devil are you doing here? You are supposed to be in court delivering those files!"

"I believe the time has come to stop 'supposing' a great deal of things," retorted Carmen. "First of all, you are going to tell me exactly what happened to that poor girl… And at the same time, you're going tell me what happened to Julian Daniel Andrade. Quite a lot of people have mysteriously disappeared where you and your cronies have been poking your noses so, either you tell me right here and now precisely what you all have been up or I'm going straight to the press."

There was a tense silence as Carrasco observed her without saying a word, while Carmen felt a sudden rush of blood to her head. He then looked down, smiling to himself, and slowly pulled a cigarette out of a packet that had been lying on his desk, before lighting up. Inhaling the smoke, he stared across the street through the wooden Venetian blinds, casting his eyes towards the vacant pavement space formerly occupied by Forero, the paraplegic shoe shiner who, until recently, had been a visible part of the colourful tapestry of the street life around the headquarters.

"Carmen, people disappear every day in this town."

Hearing the ominous sentence being uttered so casually from her superior's lips, Carmen felt she was in the lions' den. Exhaling another puff of cigarette smoke, Carrasco continued: "The thing with you is you have an attitude problem. Always getting involved in things that don't concern you. Now you want to go to the press, well, go ahead and go to the damn press… What you'll find is you'll get yourself labelled a crank. What everyone is going to realise is just how batshit crazy you are… If I were you, I would be more worried about your future. You are alone and soon you'll find yourself isolated. You have absolutely nobody willing to stick out their neck for you."

While Carrasco was talking, Carmen's fierce composure did not in the slightest betray the whirlwind of emotions nor the fear that was now beginning to build up inside her, even when she could feel the blood in her veins turning into ice. Carrasco's final words, however, felt like a punch in her gut. "Not even for that son of yours that you're trying to keep wrapped in cotton wool." With a triumphal smirk, Carrasco produced from his desk the front page of the local newspaper reporting on the drawing contest bearing her son's photograph at the award's ceremony.

Aghast and petrified, Carmen was unable to remember an occasion when Carrasco had referred so specifically to her son, and immediately began to wonder if the Lieutenant could possibly be aware of the boy's whereabouts. She felt cornered, vulnerable and infinitely small. For Carmen, there was nothing in life more precious than her son's safety and she now found herself having to face the horrific possibility that Miguel Ángel might also become part of a deadly game in which the smaller pieces were being made to disappear at a rapid rate.

CHAPTER 11

The Machinery

Late April, 1977

By break of dawn, with her thoughts in disarray but still determined not to lose sight of the urgency with which she had to act, Carmen began to explore the possibility of convening a press conference in order to publicise the events of the last 24 hours linked to Georgiana's disappearance and to that of at least two other individuals. She found herself trying to piece together the elements of a huge and complex puzzle in her addled mind while the taxi taking her along one of the city's main thoroughfares headed for Radio Galeón.

Her exit from the headquarters of the F-2 had been a precipitous and desperate manoeuvre. After walking away from the Lieutenant's office she had made for the tiny room that for more than a year had served as her personal space, where she kept very few mementoes worth rescuing, save for her son's photograph and the brown folder in which she had been compiling all manner of irregularities unearthed in the official archives office. She left behind her trusty typewriter from her days in the army in the middle of her desk, and never once looked back as she left her office for the last time and hurried towards the main entrance.

During the sleepless night that followed she pondered on the few options she had available. Her first thought was of approaching the offices of *El Informador*, but she soon ruled out that possibility when she realised she had no acquaintances at the newspaper she could fully trust. The memory of her son's photograph printed on its front page still haunted her thoughts alongside the horrifying episode in the office bathroom, concluding with the chilling showdown at Carrasco's office. However, despite her apprehensions, she knew she had to act quickly. At the same time, an equally troubling possibility was the likelihood of links between members of the F-2 and the local press. The mere thought of inadvertently jeopardising her son's safety by making the wrong move filled her with terror. Instead, she examined the possibilities of more swift and direct methods of publicising her macabre discovery.

The independent local radio station Radio Galeón was the brainchild of journalist Aurelio Carbonell Estrada, a longtime friend of Carmen's who in the space of just two years had set notable standards in investigative journalism with a broadcasting space known as "Mi Radio Periódico". Carbonell Estrada had built up a dedicated following among the wider population of the Magdalena region, most notably with a jaunty radio segment known as "Notas y Micronotas", capturing the public's imagination with its hard-hitting reportage and satirical exposure of all manner of abuses in Santa Marta's socio-political sphere.

The radio station's offices were located within a small building in the city centre, which they shared with a broadcasting corporation known as Caracol. Aurelio, in his characteristic square glasses, eagerly offered Carmen a chair and a cup of coffee as soon as she came in. Within the same white-walled room and sitting next to the audio mixer console was her lawyer, Marco Vinicio Suárez, who had answered Carmen's earlier call to be present during the transmission.

During a brief commercial break, Aurelio approached her with a warm smile: "It's good that you could get here on time". He paused: "Are you sure you want to do this?"

"I've never been surer of anything in my life," she replied.

The lawyer, who was an old friend of Carmen's, placed a hand on her shoulder in a gesture of support. "Just remember, you can choose to remain anonymous. There is no need to tell the world who you are."

"We'll see how it goes", she answered.

With the engaging verbiage that characterised his all too familiar presentation, Aurelio introduced the radio slot while, in an adjacent seat, Carmen steadied her nerves before the start of the interview. Once the cue was given for her to speak into the microphone, she proceeded to say in a clear voice:

"First of all I want to thank you for the opportunity to be here, because what I am about to declare before the community is not something I feel able to do through the local press. My name is Carmen Monzón and I currently serve as an officer of the F-2. However, I have firm reason to believe that several of my colleagues in law enforcement perpetrated the kidnapping, murder and disappearance of an innocent young tourist from abroad, a crime which has not been reported in the media. This same group of officers have also been involved in the disappearance of at least two more individuals still unaccounted for. For now, I only have the verbal testimony of two F-2 officials who gave themselves away in a verbal exchange when they believed they weren't being heard… Soon afterwards, when I attempted to seek clarification from my boss Lieutenant Carrasco regarding that discovery, my superior instead issued a direct verbal threat against me whilst I was in his office…"

As Carmen continued talking, the two men exchanged uneasy glances. The interview continued for two more minutes.

During the break, Aurelio could barely conceal his concern as he took Carmen aside: "It pains me to have to tell you this but I strongly recommend you start to make arrangements in order to leave the country. From now on, your life will be in grave danger. You know as well as I there is no way you can win with these people."

The forty-eight hours that ensued were a stream of feverish activity. During that compressed time, mother ensured she maintained regular contact with grandma and me by phone. There were a number of personal matters still requiring her immediate attention in anticipation of the storm that her radio interview had unleashed. Chief amongst these was leaving our house for safety reasons. Other priorities preying on her mind were the ongoing administration of alternative sources of income, namely the running of the farm near the Sierra Nevada, as well as the small fleet of four yellow taxis that she ran to supplement her income; these businesses would from then on have to be handled remotely and with the greatest discretion.

While the radio interview had managed to relieve the enormous burden she bore, she was under no illusion that such a bold move would be without repercussions. Despite the uncertainty that now gnawed at her insides and the feeling she was in increasingly unknown territory, she held on firmly to the belief that her decision, akin to a pawn initiating its first movement on an existential chessboard, represented a huge step forward in the grand scheme of things.

Meanwhile, in the sanctuary of his office, a grim faced Carrasco stared in silence at the wall in front of him, having received unwelcome news of the radio interview from one of his henchmen. It had not come as a complete surprise to him. He did, however, marvel at the speed with which this development had transpired. He mulled over the extent of the revelations for no more than a couple of minutes before deciding to make a phone call.

"Hello Gustavo, there is a small problem I need you to help me with".

Many hours later, once alone in the privacy of her room, Carmen felt the minutes turning to hours and became aware of a deafening silence: no telephone calls had been forthcoming. Perhaps because she felt the onslaught of loneliness more intensely than ever before, or maybe because she just felt the need to hear a friendly familiar voice, she decided to phone Tamara Escovedo, the headmistress of my school.

"Doña Tamara is not home", the housekeeper intoned impassively over the line.

"Jacinta, could you please tell her to return my call as soon as she gets home?"

"Yes, I will, madam."

A strange suspicion seized Carmen as she put down the receiver. She quickly dialled the home number of Manuelita Montero, executive of Cajamag, one of her closest associates and the person who had been instrumental in arranging her contract for the distribution of dairy and poultry products from her farm to some of the city's choicest supermarkets.

"Good evening Rosita., Could you kindly put me through to Doña Manuelita?"

"Who's calling, please?"

"Rosita, it's me, Carmen Monzón…"

"Doña Manuelita isn't at home."

"I see. Could you ask her to return my call as soon as she gets home, please?"

"Yes, madam, I will."

During the course of the evening, Carmen dialled the numbers again at regular intervals, but received the same monotonous response from both housekeepers. She felt an uneasy chill in her veins as she proceeded to call over half a dozen of her closest contacts only to receive almost identical responses.

The last Friday of the month of April arrived just like any other Friday that she could remember. For more than seventeen years she had made the same trip to the local government building to collect her salary, along with the throng of other civil servants who made a similar pilgrimage from other government departments for their monthly wages. The local government operated within the bowels of a stately yellow colonial building backing onto the notorious 13th Street. It bordered the enormous Plaza Bolívar, casting its shadow on small streets of the historic centre of the city where street vendors and the incessant swing of local citizens and tourists kept alive the small town's hustle and bustle.

Walking up the wide set of stone steps, she entered the waiting room where government staff gathered to wait for their pay, until her turn was called. Arriving at the window, Carmen greeted the lady usual, but she merely replied with a terse *"Buenas tardes"* and avoided eye contact as she handed an envelope to her through the opening in the barrier.

Exiting the payments office, and before she had got down the stairs to the exit, Carmen opened the envelope. Instead of her salary, it contained a typed letter declaring her dismissal with immediate effect, and stating that she was no longer affiliated with any government department. There was no mention of her former roles within the Ministry of Finance and Departmental Customs Guard, nor of her occupation as auditor in the Licorera of the Department in Gaira. Neither was there any acknowledgment of her transfer to the Córdova Battalion Number Five, nor the Statutory Decree through which she had been appointed as officer of the F-2. In the blink of an eye, she felt the entire weight of the state machinery crashing down on her and the effect was forceful and devastating. It brought back memories of when, as a child, she was bitten in her ankle by a coral snake while wandering around her childhood farm high in the Sierra Nevada and only the prompt intervention of her botanist father had narrowly saved her life. As she attempted to assimilate the traumatic new development, a slow-acting poison now seemed to course unimpeded through her veins. While she had always looked back upon the former event of her early childhood as just one of those things in life, the latter felt like a rip in the fabric of reality.

Tying up loose ends, her initial impulse was to return to the Government building to argue her case but she quickly realised it would be futile. The letter in her hand bore an official rubberstamp from the highest echelons, unambiguously stating her dismissal had been actioned by a resolution and signed by the acting mayor of the Department of Magdalena.

Numb and dejected, she spent hours drifting alone in a stupor, absentmindedly clutching the piece of paper in her hand. People passed her by as she wandered aimlessly through the narrow colonial streets of the city. At the end of her long walk, she found herself at the waterfront, with the incoming waves crashing onto the shore. With tears welling in her eyes, she observed an enormous crimson sun painting the skies with striking fiery red tones as it set over the Caribbean Sea.

CHAPTER 12

The Ice

Early May, 1977

Grandmother's yellow house was located in a sleepy village called Mamatoco, where time seemed to have stood still and which previously could only be accessed through an ancient thoroughfare that envoys from the Spanish crown had built to speed up the colonisation of America. No other house in the village had so much land attached to it but, despite its size, the house was a humble edifice with walls made of *bareque*, a traditional building technique involving a combination of wood and mud that helped houses stay cool in the heat, stabilised by a thick wooden roofing structure topped with a zinc roof. The house appeared to have endured the passage of centuries. I could run freely inside it and continue running uninterrupted through its open and vast back yard, amidst tropical trees that provided a habitat to myriad varieties of North Atlantic wildlife. It was also a place where one could just as easily be lulled to sleep by the sound of birdsong on lazy afternoons as be kept awake at night by thunderous rain hitting the corrugated zinc roof during raging tropical storms.

Earlier that day, and over the course of my stay at the yellow house, grandmother had remembered why she found certain habits of mine bordering on intolerable, such as my playing with my food and feeding choice portions from my lunch to the pets, not to mention my spontaneous compulsion for drawing figures in the air whilst sitting at the table. In fairness to her, she was probably terrified her two elderly guardian dogs were going to chomp off my fingers along with the morsels from my plate that I kept dangling so invitingly before their eager faces.

Despite being over eighty years of age, grandmother was the ubiquitous engine that kept the yellow house in functioning order. The veteran of two strokes, the last of which had immobilised one side of her face, she had not slowed down one iota, and her perennial and incessant schedule of housekeeping ensured every nook and cranny of that vast edifice was spotlessly clean. This included all the laundry that she gathered from the house's four residents, which included two of grandmother's siblings and myself, consisting of everyday clothes, ladies' fineries, towels and bedcovers that she personally washed by hand and hung out to dry unassisted all along the backyard, barely drawing breath before getting back to work cooking lunch for both humans and an assorted coterie of domesticated animals.

It was felt by all that I was beginning to spend far too much time in the room where grandmother kept all her religious icons and devotional images, These included a vast array of saints and yellowed lithographs of different versions of the Virgin Mary, images of beatific European women dressed in pastel-coloured robes, all dimly lit by candles that endowed the space with a golden Byzantine glow. Among that same pantheon of saints and martyrs from Christendom was a particular one grandmother called '*la virgen*', holding court in the middle of a dark grotto, resplendent in ultramarine blue and surrounded by two infants crawling around a glowing angel. Every time I wandered into that room I felt I was leaving the twentieth century behind. I stood before depictions of women so far removed from my limited sphere of perception and of such unattainable celestial reality that they surely inhabited a dimension inaccessible to mortals.

Mesmerised by the women's long bodies and slender hands, some with improbably blue eyes like those of Georgiana, the most outlandish possibility momentarily occurred to me: what if mother had actually brought a flesh-and-blood version of one of these otherworldly beings to our house and she had been living with us under the same roof all along?

In order to avoid spending too much time in that room or being forever distracted among the fruit trees in the back yard or being endlessly fascinated by rows of ants working in unison as they carried off remaining bits of food I left for them in the dining room and, most of all, to preserve whatever tranquility had formerly been enjoyed by the inhabitants of the house prior to my arrival, it was decided that I be taken out for a walk by a group of high school students from the village who often ran errands for my grandmother in order for me to take part in more conventional distractions.

A five-minute walk from the house, through a park lined with tall trupillo trees, was the Quinta de San Pedro Alejandrino, a place popular with secondary education and university students. This sumptuously decorated nineteenth-century hacienda had belonged to a wealthy Spanish supporter of Colombia's independence, and one Saturday afternoon I was being treated to a history tour about the last days in the life of El Libertador Simón Bolívar, the general who had liberated five South American countries from the yoke of Spanish rule – and the antithesis of his contemporary Napoleon Bonaparte who reinstated slavery in all French Caribbean colonies before crowning himself emperor of France.

"This is the room where Simon Bolívar died", the elderly custodian showing us around explained. Next to Bolívar's bed, which was covered by a massive Colombian flag, were two red velvet chairs and a clock that had been stopped for posterity at exactly one o'clock and three minutes, the very moment the Liberator had drawn his last breath.

As my custodian and I walked through the hacienda's orange and lemon trees and circumvented the enormous white arched monument that they called El Altar de La Patria, he recounted the anecdote of the daring robbery of Bolivar's sword carried out by the subversive group M-19 just a couple of years earlier.

"Why would they steal a sword?", I asked.

The reply, which was immediately forthcoming, was more than a little unsettling: "Maybe they took the sword because there wasn't a child from Bolívar's family that they could kidnap in order to demand a ransom."

Back in November, and to everyone's surprise, the local newspaper *El Informador* had published a photo of me being flanked by two runners-up from other schools, standing together on a makeshift podium in a building near Santa Marta's cathedral where the awards ceremony had taken place. The surprise was partly due to the fact that the relatively sedate piece of good news on the front page represented a welcome departure from the endless streak of dire headlines reporting events such as the bloody vendetta incessantly raging between the infamous Cárdenas and Valdeblánquez clans, as well as daily protests undertaken by students from Liceo Celedón.

"Your mum will be very pleased," I remember my great-uncle commenting in the living room of the yellow house as he flicked through a late November edition of the newspaper. "It's not every day that *El Informador* decides to publish happy news on its front page for a change."

The trophy I was awarded featured a brass miniature of a winged victory on a wooden pedestal. When placed atop grandmother's television set, it proved to be far more effective in correcting the appliance's picture quality than the aerial itself.

As it turned out, however, mother did not share in any of the jubilation that the headline had provoked, neither in my school nor at my grandmother's household.

Returning from Quinta De San Pedro Alejandrino, mother's unexpected presence in my grandmother's house immediately filled me with joy and happiness. She was casually dressed in blue jeans and a short-sleeved linen shirt, clothes she would normally wear for a weekend trip to the farm. My momentary elation was followed by the realisation that all was not well, as I detected a fleeting sense of anguish in her countenance that she attempted to conceal without success. Both grandmother and the others sat in the living room without saying a word and a sense of unease hung over the room like a heavy cloud. Placing both her hands on my shoulders and looking me warmly in the eye, mother said: "Son, you and I are going on a trip to the capital. We'll be going to the airport first thing tomorrow. I bought you some new clothes so you won't feel the cold on the plane."

Her words appeared to herald a significant change in our circumstances and a sense that life for us would never be the same again. My initial reaction was to wonder how I was going to process the idea of an imminent trip to the capital as I had never before been so far away from home. Despite a tingling sensation in my ears and what felt like a swarm of butterflies fluttering in my stomach, the reality was I had missed my mother's presence all the days I had spent in the yellow house. What anchored me to the moment was the certainty that, whatever the immediate future held for us, she would be by my side in the coming days.

However, the feeling that something was not quite as it should be was as palpable as the embrace I then received from her. The sombre facial expressions and the silent exchange of looks among those sitting in the room spoke volumes. Above all, the usual conversations that would normally ensue between adults when I was in their midst were now conspicuously absent.

The many errands that mother had to carry out before our trip included a private face-to-face meeting between her and Tamara Escovedo, the principal of my elementary school. I had been expected to complete my primary education that year but now ad-hoc arrangements were swiftly being made behind closed doors to ensure my studies could continue uninterrupted in an alternative school in Bogotá. San Isidro de Toledo operated in a large private property adjacent to Avenida Libertador and right in front of El Jardín, one of Santa Marta's most tranquil and coveted neighbourhoods. We arrived there in one of the yellow taxis that were part of a small fleet of vehicles that mother ran as a business and with which she supplemented her income. While my mother met with the principal in private, the security employee instructed to keep an eye on me took me on a swift tour of the now empty classrooms where my schoolmates and I had been given lessons in history, arithmetic, religion, botany and geography. I was also granted a final view of the large leisure room on the ground floor where over the years mother had been given permission to organise my earliest birthday parties. Because I requested it, the ad hoc tour also included a quick visit to the library, my favourite space in the entire school, used almost exclusively by the principal and her family, where books by classic American authors and works of European literature had first come to my attention, the same room where I had learned to play my first board games and the place I would sometimes use as my personal refuge from the noise of the playground.

For some reason, I was not allowed to wander freely through the large courtyard of the campus where my colleagues and I had used to gather during break times. My presence there that morning had coincided with a festival in full progress at the back of the school with all students in attendance, an event which included the participation of entertainers such as 'Uncle Memo' the Magician and other acts dressed as clowns mingling with students in the patio terrace. And so it was that I wistfully watched part of the afternoon's proceedings through the bars of a window on the second floor, as classmates I had grown up with stood gathered in their uniforms singing hymns and nursery rhymes that we had all learned together in the shade of the mango and lemon trees. To be allowed to watch them from above as just an observer was a decidedly strange feeling. However, the circumstances rapidly unfolding around me had left me suspecting that many wishes would remain unfulfilled and many words would remain unspoken.

Little did I suspect this would be the very last time I would see those sky-blue uniforms or that I would never return to my old school again.

Second week of May, 1977

At daybreak the following day, the taxi driver put the luggage in the boot of the car while our relatives in the house hugged us both farewell. I remember very little about the occasion because it was very early in the morning and I was already immersed in that intermediate state of mind that's said to exist between goodbyes and final destinations. While the taxi took us to Simón Bolívar airport and mother talked to me about clothes and school notebooks, I watched the panoramic strip of the Caribbean Sea beneath a cloudless horizon and a long series of wooden beach huts that flicked past in quick succession as we left the city behind.

While we waited to board the plane for Bogotá, I stood on the viewing deck watching in complete fascination the way those gigantic flying machines made a mockery of gravity, the roar of the turbines reminding me of the extended sound of thunder during the tropical rainstorms that had so often kept me awake at night. Once airborne, I gazed out the cabin window at the immensity of the Caribbean Sea, its sparkling blue waters glinting in the morning sun. The aircraft tilted and swerved in mid-air above the sea before gathering speed over the mountain range of the Andes, and setting course towards the unknown. I became entranced by the spectacle of clouds looking exactly like cotton flakes passing our window at breakneck speed. Mum had already ensured I was wearing several layers of clothing in anticipation of the glacial cold that would soon be greeting us in the capital.

The first thing that struck me, apart from the constant bursts of sharp cold air buffeting my face outside the airport, was the enormous contrast between the sunny atmosphere we had left behind in the Atlantic coast and the damp, lugubrious metropolis I would be calling home for the foreseeable future, where everyone walked in too much of a hurry wearing heavy dark clothing, under an inclement gloomy drizzle. The backlog of traffic seemed interminable as the vehicle taking us to our destination struggled to move along the damp roads.

When we finally reached our destination I glanced through the window at our temporary residence, a single-storey house on the corner of a desolate-looking neighbourhood where every area was paved or covered in dimly-lit concrete. We accessed the property through a corridor with olive green walls, which gave onto an atrium which in turn led to three bedrooms, a bathroom and a kitchen. The owners of the premises, the Buitrago family, were relatives of Felipe Peláez, one of my primary school classmates. Mother had managed to establish telephone contact with the family through Julia, Felipe's older sister, to arrange my accommodation following emergency talks between mother and my headmistress back in Santa Marta that ultimately resulted in my enrolment in a little-known school in Bogotá where I was to be taught for the remainder of my primary education.

Julia had been waiting for our arrival by the entrance and quickly led us to our room where mum soon emptied our suitcase and set out to organising the contents in a wardrobe. Mum made a sustained effort to make me feel as comfortable as she humanly could in the midst of the enormous change unfolding in our lives.

Leaving behind for a moment the activity in our room, my eyes turned towards something small scurrying through the edge of the atrium. It was a lonely quail, ceaselessly running up and down a narrow strip of vegetation around the edge of the internal courtyard, seemingly unable to find a place where it could stop to get some rest.

Federico, one of Eliécer Buitrago's two sons, was the same age as me, while Tomás was a year older. Displaying the marked decorum and politeness that was said to characterise the people of Bogotá, the two boys showed me around the house and then invited me to sit with them in the living room, in front of a huge TV set broadcasting programs on Channel Two, while their mother and Julia prepared dinner.

The next day, while mum held a meeting with the family to discuss and agree on the budget for my maintenance and school expenses, I was back in the atrium sharing some breadcrumbs left over from my breakfast with the lonely quail. I often distracted myself with activities that disconnected me from whatever was happening in the adult would around me. I had a maxim for adults: while I respectfully understood they should be heard, I also believed they should be seen as little as possible. Most of all, I considered that there was always a dividing line between adult matters, where everything seemed to vary constantly, and my private world where things made far more sense.

One morning about a week after we arrived, mum woke me very early. Parting the curtains, she got me look through the window of our room and for the first time in my life I witnessed a hailstorm in full progress. I knelt on my bed open mouthed as the ice descended noisily from the sky, bouncing off the glass and covering the outside urban landscape in white. That same weekend, she took me to see an event at the Coliseo El Campín, a large entertainment venue in the capital. I vividly recall a show called *Disney on Parade*, in which classic movie characters were brought to life by costumed professional skaters on a vast ice rink with the most elaborate props and exquisite scenery. We all gasped in amazement as an army of chimney sweepers swerved around the ice at dizzying speed and a gigantic animation of Mary Poppins singing *A Spoonful of Sugar* was projected against a large backdrop screen, the tune of the song becoming instantly etched in my memory. The highlight of the night for me was seeing Peter Pan in full flight, wearing his distinctive green leaves forest attire under glaring multicoloured lights, soaring to lofty heights with the help of invisible wires, leaving in his wake a trail of silver stars against the backdrop of Big Ben – an episode that would rekindle my conception of London as a place of magic and wonderment. The event concluded with what appeared to be snow falling from the sky like a cascade of shimmering cotton flakes. It was a memorable and life-affirming evening that washed away my worries if only for one day, and yet another occasion when mum seemed to have the power to conjure up the impossible.

Despite the persistently confusing family dynamics of a house with five constantly interactive family members who argued a lot, I was nonetheless aware of frequent and discreet telephone calls that mum kept making on a daily basis, in addition to telegrams that regularly kept arriving at the address, until one day a courier on a bicycle showed up at the door of the house carrying an urgent message that appeared to be key in mum's decision to return to Santa Marta. As shocked as I was at the unexpected prospect of her leaving without as much as a warning, I remained confident that whatever the nature of the 'adult matter' at hand, it was surely something she was quite capable of resolving in her own time, even if my curious mind was struggling to join the dots as to what exactly could be unravelling. It did not help matters that I was as yet unable to grasp the complexity of mum being forced to run two fixed sources of income from afar. Even if her imminent departure from Bogotá so soon after our recent trip had taken me by surprise, her presence back in Santa Marta was imperative for the continuing functioning of her business interests.

During one of the few days of uninterrupted light that I remember seeing in the capital, she took me along with her to an open market on a shopping trip to ensure I had lots to eat in her absence, as well as to contribute to the family's food stock. The night before her flight we both sang the badly misconstrued lyrics to *A Spoonful of Sugar* while in bed, as best as we both could remember them. She urged me to remain calm as I struggled to adjust to the new environment in my temporary home and encouraged me to continue being the exemplary student I had always been back at my old school. She also left me with a promise of more sunny days to be enjoyed back home, more early mornings milking cows in our farm and more bingeing on tropical fruit in the gigantic backyard of my grandmother's big yellow house. As she whispered in my ear, I closed my eyes and visualised her words in my mind's eye and in perfect CinemaScope, feeling weightless and liberated, like a soap bubble gently floating in the warmth of an afternoon sun. Her last words were uttered with the certainty of someone accustomed to fulfilling her promises to the letter, even if they were tinged with an eager tenderness disguising troubling truths that could not be expressed. Before I fell asleep in her arms, I had no doubt that, at the end of an already convoluted journey, we would soon be back together again.

The school I had been enrolled in, Joaquín Caicedo, operated in a nondescript industrial building comprising two echoey concrete floors without a recreational patio and whose harsh halogen lighting illuminated its classrooms with a sickly artificial gloom. As I entered each classroom I was assigned to attend, the immediate contrast to what I had grown used to in my former school was summarised by the complete absence of women teachers. Outside the classroom, the overall atmosphere was frantic and fast-paced and students always seemed to be in a perpetual hurry as they raced up and down the stairs without pause. At this early stage of my new student phase, my main moral support was the presence of the two brothers who had initially made a point of watching over me as I tried to acclimatise to my new environment in as seamless a fashion as possible, before they decided I had spread my wings sufficiently to manage the vagaries of school life on my own.

Speaking of novelties, I soon discovered that being 'from the coast', particularly when speaking with my *costeño* accent, automatically marked me among my peers as someone who was deemed to be 'different'. This was compounded by the fact that, back in the day, encountering people from the northern part of the country living and studying in certain parts of the capital was still a relatively rare occurrence, most of all for those who were of a young age. And while I perceived benevolence and good intentions from the odd inquisitive lecturer, I was painfully aware of being little more than a novelty to those who chose to watch me from a distance or had conversations with me just to hear my accent. Immersing myself in reading, therefore, became a necessity in times of distress and even in the most difficult of circumstances I always ensured I had a book in hand to fill any time spent on my own. Looking back, I regretted no longer having access to anything like my beloved primary school library, a place I had so often chosen as my private refuge away from the din of school life.

To make matters worse, my new teachers were soon perplexed by my increasingly poor academic results. Indeed, my performance in class had become so dismal that the excellent grades attributed to the *costeño* boy from San Isidro de Toledo might as well have been achieved by a completely different student. In this uncharted grey-toned reality of my waking hours, my instinctive response was to try to soldier on from day to day, hoping I could learn something valuable from the experience while a succession of colourless and empty days devoid of any meaning continued to unfold around me. Relying on a survival instinct I had no inkling I possessed and in my stubborn resolution to withstand the cold without complaining or explaining, I had failed to detect the first stirrings of instability quietly germinating within me like a tiny seed.

In the course of the days that followed mum's departure, for the first time in my life I began to be overwhelmed by a burgeoning sensation of panic. Sleeping at night had become a near impossibility and a sensation like someone placing a large heavy brick on my chest exacerbated my asthma symptoms, constraining my breathing until the pressure had become so extreme that I ended up convincing myself the best survival strategy lay in the possibility of running away and finding a way to rejoin my mother.

Wide awake in the middle of a long cold night and with my breath turning into visible puffs of white steam, I silently sneaked out of my room and walked along the freezing concrete floor in the dark, clutching the case of crayons I had been awarded as a prize in that fateful art competition a few weeks earlier. At the forefront of my mind – doubtless the result of a multitude of sleepless nights blurring the division between a stark reality and the escapism afforded by didactic games we used to play as wide eyed students in our history lessons – lay the tantalising possibility of 'portals' as a means of gaining freedom from a stifling and desperate situation. Propelled by an overriding sense of hope and nostalgia, the concept of being transported through one of these 'portals' back to a different place in space and time suddenly did not seem as absurd or even beyond the bounds of probability.

Locking myself in the bathroom and turning on the light, I proceeded to draw a door on one of the walls, the condensation on the surface endowing the pigments with the texture of wet tempera as the crayons glided across the tiles. Applying the finishing touches, I scribbled the words 'Santa Marta' in big capital letters above the 'portal', as high as my arms could reach.

73

Exhausted by the effort, I returned to my room and for the first time in many nights, fell into a deep sleep.

The next day I felt the big strong hands of an adult dragging me out of bed, forcibly leading me through the atrium and into the bathroom under the stunned gaze of all members of the household who had already woken up on that cold morning. Incandescent with rage and holding the back of my neck in a vice-like grip, the father of the kids pushed my face close to the wall and forced me to look at the 'portal' I had painted with crayons on the tiles, threatening to smash my face in. Mercifully, the timely intervention of his wife, combined with loud protestations from other members of the family prevented a more regrettable outcome.

The days passed and life in the house carried on without further incident, although it continued to be routinely cold and drab. My longstanding bouts of anxiety were replaced by an overall feeling of numbness. Even reading, my favourite pastime, became a chore and my only delight now was feeding leftovers from my food to the lonely quail quietly relegated to its narrow strip of grass, and who seemed invisible to the other inhabitants of the house.

The brothers gradually introduced me to the world of trading cards, and evenings were spent watching television huddled together on the living room carpet. During long commercial breaks we would blow into the air to see whose breath created the longer lasting cloud of vapour. We entertained ourselves with a staple of programs such as *Zorro*, *Animalandia* and *Sábados Felices*, but I always made a point of pausing our clowning around whenever the Colman's mustard advert came on. I would watch its various stock black-and-white images of London and quite soon, memories of Georgiana, her Big Ben and her Changing of the Guard would come flooding back to me from a much happier time. I then found myself hoping that the intrepid traveler who had once upon a time foretold my coming to England was safe and happy in her faraway land of gigantic clocks.

CHAPTER 13

On the Run

Late June, 1977

After almost an hour of turbulence flying from the capital back to Santa Marta, the plane touched down on the runway of Simón Bolívar airport with an audible skid on the asphalt. One of the drivers from the small taxi fleet managed by my mother caught sight of Julia and I in the arrivals lounge, having just retrieved our luggage from the conveyor belt. We got in the car, a black and beige Dodge Dart urban regulation taxi that could carry up to six passengers, and swiftly set course for the yellow house near San Pedro Alejandrino where grandma was eagerly awaiting our arrival. Having given me a prolonged embrace that left almost no air in my lungs, she quietly relayed news to Julia, discreetly handing her a handwritten note of instructions the driver needed to follow. It became apparent a plan B was in progress and that we were to be driven from the house to an unfamiliar alternative address. The realisation I would not get to enjoy grandma's back yard for even one minute filled me with frustration.

We then headed towards El Alambique, one of the smallest and most confined neighbourhoods of the city, advancing slowly along an unpaved road full of potholes. In my hands I clutched a plastic folder containing my primary school certificate from Joaquin Caicedo school, along with a colour picture of Peter Pan that I had drawn for mum before my trip. During the journey, I thought of different ways I would announce the happy news of my graduation in Bogotá to my mother and became so impatient to see her that an incessant sensation of butterflies fluttering in my stomach had me giddy with excitement.

The headlights of the vehicle were the only source of light as we entered the sector, which had run out of electricity due to yet another blackout. It was a suffocating night laden with heavy clouds. While the crunching noise of tires on stones reverberated in our ears, Julia once again read out the address to the taxi driver from mum's handwritten note. Finally, the taxi stopped right in front of one nondescript house with no front porch making up a long row of properties where no one appeared to be living. Julia instructed the taxi driver to stay put, as, according to the note, he would be needed for one more errand.

Upon entering the house, an elderly woman dressed in black who was in the process of lighting a kerosene lamp, hastily offered us a seat in the living room while Julia helped bring my luggage in. Fiddling with the wick to increase the light in the room, the old lady approached me, speaking so close to my face that I could smell coffee on her breath: "Come with me. Your mum is desperate to see you." More excited than ever by the prospect of seeing my mum again and still clutching the plastic folder containing the drawing and my school notes in my sweaty hands, I followed the lady through a set of interior curtains into a gloomy, cavernous room where the colour of the walls could barely be seen.

The air in the windowless room was heavy and stale, filling one's lungs with a musty sadness. The lamp carried by the lady shed sufficient light through the gloom for us to cast moving shadows around us, until my eyes were finally able to distinguish a motionless mound lying on a single bed. For a moment, a tortuous wheezing sound was all that could be heard in the room.

"*Ave María purísima*", the old lady exclaimed under her breath as she gently but nervously ushered me in. Standing by the bed was a svelte young woman, whom I assumed was a nurse as boxes of medicines and a jug of water became visible on a bedside table by a motionless electric fan.

A chill ran down my spine as I saw mum bowing her head down over the side of the bed and proceeding to vomit a thick substance into a bucket placed on the floor. As I stepped backwards in horror, the light from the kerosene lamp caused our silhouettes to be projected onto the walls of the room, my mother's body overcome by convulsions. Unable to say a word, I watched petrified in the half-light while she continued to cough noisily for what seemed like an eternity. When the room had finally fallen silent, the nurse stepped aside and announced in a quavering voice: "Señora, your son is here to see you."

Finally, mum looked up and addressed me weakly, with a disturbing crackle in her voice that made her sound ancient.

"My boy, I'm so happy to see you. How was your trip?"

I was unable to say a word as I observed her cracked lips and pallid, emaciated features close up.

Momentarily recovering a measure of composure, she mustered some energy to reassure me. "Please, please try not to worry… I've been a little sick but I'm already feeling so much better… It's all going to be better tomorrow. And I'm sorry I can't hug you right now but I just don't want you to come down with a cold… I assure you that from tomorrow you and I will be making up for lost time".

Turning unsteadily to the lady in black, she then requested I be shown to my room so I could get some rest. Before leaving the chamber, I reached out to touch mum's arm and felt her burning with a high fever.

The torrential downpour that broke out in the night ensured my sleep was scarce and my thoughts were once again filled with worry and uncertainty. As dawn broke, the day found me sitting in the lounge area contemplating the street turning into a raging river that threatened to enter the house through the front door, dragging all manner of debris in its muddy, turbulent waters.

Despite the fact that the electricity service had been restored in the neighbourhood and lights were back on, the telephone lines remained down and no communication with the outside world was possible. Meanwhile, mum was already in the kitchen preparing breakfast and cooking a massive pot of stew to last us all for the rest of the day, giving me a smile at every opportunity and assuring me that she was feeling much better. Despite her glimmer of optimism, though, it was not long before she returned to her darkened room, where she was to remain convalescing for a further forty-eight hours.

By then the waters had subsided enough to allow some of the neighbourhood's few inhabitants to leave their houses in order to shop for provisions. Throughout those days of endless rain I entertained myself in my room making a Peter Pan doll for mom, painstakingly cutting and gluing leaves of the forest to make his costume out of fragments of green suede paper left over from my school handicraft lessons. I then quietly sneaked into mum's bedroom and carefully fixed the doll onto the headrest of her bed with some glue.

By early evening mum felt well enough to join us at the table. On the sideboard there was crackly old transistor radio broadcasting the evening news as if from outer space, assisted by Lazarus-like batteries that somehow still powered the tattered appliance. Mostly out of boredom, I filtered out the crackly noise from the radio and in reducing the volume found myself eavesdropping on the conversation between the two women. I came to realise that mum had come to an agreement with the old lady to allow us to stay in her house on a temporary basis. She was the mother of one of mum's schoolfriends from long ago, who was now deceased. I fixed my eyes on a group of faded family photos neatly arranged in silvery frames on a counter at the side of the room. I studied with fascination the Creole features of people from yesteryear in elegant attire, bearing expressions of pride tinged with melancholy. I then noticed a more recent black-and-white photo of a group of girls wearing the uniform of La Normal de Señoritas, a girls school that had been founded in Santa Marta by German missionaries in the nineteenth century. One of the faces appeared familiar to me – that of my mother. Looking at the photo, I found it heartwarming to realise that she too had developed strong ties of friendship at school.

Because I had started getting used to the way that adults tended to codify messages, by shortening sentences or lowering the tone of their voices, when certain matters of importance arose, I could not help but briefly pick up on something about a local radio station and a certain interview that had sparked a great deal of commotion in the region. I also learned that mum had experienced a series of difficulties in my absence, not least the fact that, following an emergency trip to the farm near the Sierra Nevada, she had become stranded while trying to get back to the city, following the sudden collapse of a bridge that had been washed away during heavy downpours. She had been forced to spend several days in a remote village riddled with mosquitoes and lacking drinking water, which had resulted in her contracting dengue fever. I also gleaned that our house had been let to a family from Jamaica and that there had been difficulties in collecting the payments, which were an important source of income to my mother. As I tuned out of the conversation, I reached the conclusion that finding mum in such a deplorable state of health upon my return from a cold and distant place, having being separated from one another for so long, was the worst thing that could ever have happened.

By the end of that day, the telephone service had finally been reestablished and mum was back to making and receiving a series of calls that led to lengthy conversations. From the little I could gather, it was clear that our stay in that house was coming to an end and that new arrangements were being made for us to relocate to a new address the following morning.

That last night there, mum decided to keep me company in my room. Looking completely reinvigorated, she switched on the electric fan she had carried from her convalescent chamber, before proceeding to tickle my ribs thorough my pyjamas, as she often used to do when I was younger, reducing me to eye-watering peals of laughter that left me spent and out of breath. When all was still and all lights were out, I unburdened everything that had been occupying my mind for more than a month. Among many things, I reiterated my wish for us to get out of the city and find solace in the farm near the Sierra Nevada. I let her know how much I missed my schoolmates and wondered about the chances of my reuniting with my friends in San Luis Beltrán school, given that the start of term was fast approaching.

I never got to hear mum's response to my barrage of questions, or if she had tried to calm my anxiety in any way. I was so exhausted that I soon fell asleep while she was still talking. It had been a strange week, in which reversals of fortune continued to affect our lives and neither of us knew with any certainty where any of the emerging possibilities were taking us. I dreamt we were both passengers on a white-knuckle ride on a gigantic rollercoaster that showed no signs of slowing down.

The sound of the taxi horn woke me up when it was still dark outside. Wrenching myself out of bed, I clumsily dressed myself in the same clothes I had worn the day before while mum, who had already packed our bags, signalled through the window to the driver to wait for us a little longer. It was evident she had not wanted to wake me, aware of just how much the sleepless nights had exhausted me. I ran out to meet her in the vehicle with the engine still running in front of the house. Suddenly remembering the Peter Pan I had fixed to mum's bed, I rushed back inside to the bedroom where she had spent much of her time convalescing, as though in hiding. I made a careful effort to prise off my Peter Pan without wrecking it as the taxi driver sounded the horn again. With a final pull, I managed to free the delicate effigy and cradled it in my hands towards the waiting car. The residues of green suede paper stuck to that bedstead would have been the only physical evidence that mum and I had ever been in that house.

CHAPTER 14

The Red Light

Leaving El Alambique behind, the driver was instructed to take us to Calle de Las Piedras in Sector Norte, an area north of the city where every other house was used as hostel accommodation and the rest consisted of old bars, brothels and billiard rooms. Enforcement officers from the F-2 were known to make hit-and-run incursions into drinking establishments including cabarets popular with sailors and railway workers, amongst which were the notorious 'La Francesa' and 'Luces de Paris'.

Dawn was just beginning to break and the street felt saturated with the sound of sad bolero music. The smell of stale beer pervaded the air. The detritus on the street from the revelry of the past night slowly came into view to the sound of greenish sewer waters running down each side of the road.

This was the ideal time to arrive unnoticed, as the first rays of the sun emerged over the mountains and long after the police had finished their habitual incursions into local businesses they deemed to be fair game for disruption.

We got out of the taxi in front of a hostel without any signage and I soon found myself lying on my back on a single bed under a cobweb-covered fan which span around so fast and unevenly that I feared it might collapse from the ceiling at any moment. For her part, mum was sorting out our laundry from our suitcase.

I quickly drifted off to sleep, only to be awoken by the hostel owner's children, boys around the same age as me, running up and down the stairs and threatening to topple whoever was in their way. I wondered about mum's whereabouts. The small bed that had been assigned to us occupied more than a third of the room, which had no direct access to a sink or a bathroom. I looked at our suitcase lying on a chair and felt as though we were in an airport waiting to board another plane towards yet another unspecified location. As soon as the children had stopped playing their noisy game of snakes and ladders, I leapt out of bed and went downstairs. The reception area of the makeshift hostel consisted of a small lounge whitewashed with lime, the surface of its walls decorated by a tangle of dusty electrical cables that fed a huge television set attached to a couple of speakers fixed precariously to the wall.

Mum, who was now wearing a scarf and sunglasses, was talking on the telephone by the reception.

Standing behind her was a young woman with a coiffured hairdo whom I recognised to be the nurse I had seen by my mother's bed at the house of the lady in black. As soon as mum had put down the receiver she introduced me to Natalia, who in broad daylight was a girl of no more than twenty, looking much younger now than she had appeared in that gloomy room in El Alambique. She moved in an agile way and had an elaborate hairdo. She was dressed in casual clothes, with denim trousers that tightly hugged her slender figure.

I had very little clue as to why Natalia had become a habitual presence in our midst. I would only learn much later that the girl with the hairdo and earnest disposition had sworn loyalty to mum out of gratitude, having been one of a handful of female detainees at her place of work and whom she had chosen to assist in the face of abuse meted out by the authorities.

Mum turned to me with a smile and explained she would have to leave shortly to attend an urgent business meeting and that Natalia would be taking care of me for a couple of hours. She made me promise not leave the hostel under any circumstances until she returned. On cue, the taxi pulled over in front of the hostel and, as I watched her getting in, I felt reassured that she seemed to be so in control of the situation.

The owner of the hostel, a shirtless man with a voluminous belly, who wore a pair of bright red shorts most of the time, was almost permanently in front of the television, watching football, cigarette in hand. His considerable frame fully occupied a metal rocking chair that creaked under his weight. Meanwhile, his tireless children ran continually around the property, playing hide-and-seek in every nook and cranny of it. When the referee blew the whistle for a penalty, the man would blast out an obscenity, throw his cigarette on the floor and march off to the reception area with a gesture of disgust. As the children continued to run rings around me, I headed to the double front door of the hostel to get some fresh air. For a while I stood there, observing the pageant of local life unfolding like a colourful parade to the sound of clashing billiard balls from nearby bars.

People stood around gossiping, or playing cards and dominoes on put-up tables, while the sound of live drums from adjacent streets and music from communal speakers livened the whole community. Despite the police raids on its more notorious establishments, the street had seen very little change since the 1930s when it had become the epicentre of low-life entertainment, catering for dock workers who frequented its bars and brothels. In the process the street had acquired the nickname of "Calle de la Perdición".

My view was unexpectedly obstructed by the figure of a large man materialising out of nowhere and coming to an abrupt stop right in front of me. He carried a rucksack on his shoulder and his moustache competed with dense sideburns.

"Son, is your mum around?"

I stood petrified, unable to utter a word. The midday sun fell perpendicularly on his sweaty, pockmarked face and time seemed to have stopped as he stared at me for an uncomfortably long moment.

"Tell her I'll be coming back tomorrow."

With that, the man then headed off down the street. I cautiously watched him until he had disappeared from my field of vision. Immediately after, I ran upstairs to the bedroom where Natalia was folding our newly ironed clothes and threw myself back on the bed under the ceiling fan with its strands of revolving cobwebs, having trouble catching my breath

"You'd better stay in this room until the lady comes back," I heard Natalia say as she zipped up our suitcase.

Shortly after mum's return to the hostel, I stood in the lounge area recounting the incident of the mystery man to my mother, Natalia and the owner. This prompted the three adults to engage in a guessing game as to the man's identity. Apparently there could be countless reasons as to why anybody would want to know of mum's whereabouts and hence a more accurate description of the man was called for.

"Can you draw the man you saw at the door?" mum asked in a pleading tone.

I never forgot a face, so I immediately set out to draw the features of the stranger on a notebook they placed in front of me. For the first time since our arrival, the children had stopped running and watched every stroke I made in blue ink on the paper. When I finally put the pen down, the owner of the place snatched the notebook to study the portrait more closely. Immediately, he threw his head back and laughed: "I'll be damned if it's not Fatty Ortiz!"

He continued to laugh, his voluminous shirtless belly trembling like a blob of gelatine. "This guy always pops round to persuade my missus to buy lottery tickets. He might look scary but he's quite harmless."

Turning to mother and me, he gave us a reassuring toothy grin. "You are always in good hands with Natalia. Her friends are my friends too! Make sure you all stick around, food and drinks are on the house!"

Mother and Natalia exchanged looks as he walked away notebook in hand, still chuckling. I thought it odd that I had not seen any other women in the establishment, let alone the "missus" just alluded to by the owner. As for the women, they spoke anxiously amongst themselves. Despite the ongoing noise in the background, the gist of it was that, in some circles, street vendors had a reputation for being police informers, which presented the women with a pressing dilemma: Natalia no longer felt she could trust the owner's motivations nor his sudden eagerness to please, which seemed out of kilter with his usual behaviour. As for mum, it had not escaped her notice that F-2 operatives would often argue among themselves as to which lottery vendors were the most reliable informants. And if 'Napoleon and his operatives' could possibly fit this particular picture, then staying at the hostel for much longer could prove to be a costly miscalculation. Upon hearing the name 'Napoleon', images of blue and red toy paper soldiers filled with treats were immediately conjured up in my head while the women continued their anxious verbal exchange. Unable to establish with any certainty that the earlier incident had been anything more sinister than a case of mistaken identity, the women decided to err on the side of caution and swiftly made arrangements for us to relocate to a different address.

CHAPTER 15

The Hill

Early August, 1977

That same night, we left the hostel to the sound of Celia Cruz, the pungent smell of *aguardiente* wafting from local canteens, the melée of passers-by, and the splashing of sewage water from the bicycle wheels of groups of boys. With our suitcase in the trunk of the taxi, and with Natalia giving directions to the driver from the front passenger seat, we soon left the red-light district behind and headed for the northern edge of the city.

Several blocks on, the taxi slowed down as it passed through the more tranquil parts of a neighbourhood known as Pescaíto. Despite it being nighttime, I caught sight of locals playing football on dusty streets and small groups of people of all ages congregating on every corner. The neighbourhood had once been a village for early settlers who since the middle of the eighteenth century had made a living from fishing and from working in the local salt mines. The territory adjoined an isolated hill far from the city centre and irrigation of the area from a small river running down from a small mountain range in the east had made it possible for communities to thrive and prosper. That was until the unexpected arrival of war ships commanded by a Spaniard known as Pablo Morillo, nicknamed 'El Pacificador' who, along with eight thousand of his troops, temporarily pitched up tents in the area and used it as a garbage dump before sailing off with his men to put the city of Cartagena de Indias under a notorious siege that brought its inhabitants to the brink of starvation.

The conversation in the car revolved around reaching a safe house on the other side of the railway tracks. My schoolmates and I had often been regaled with tales of a mythical railway route that, in its glory days, was used by a legendary yellow steam train bringing its cargo all the way from the Zona Bananera plantations to the seaport. The car slowed down as we reached the limits of the urban perimeter, where the railway line lay some twenty yards ahead of us, on the other side of a recently built motorway.

"Are we going to watch the yellow train, mum? I really wouldn't want to miss it!"

"Not tonight, my dear. For the time being, were going to wait for the right moment to cross over to the other side…"

An even more hushed and tentative conversation resumed between the adults and it became clear that mother and I were once again about to venture into the unknown. Ahead of us, a bank of earth running parallel to the railway line hampered the passage of the car into the hills and only heavy-tonnage vehicles could drive over the steep mound of earth without risking potential damage. Our taxi had come to a halt at a junction of the northern motorway and, for a moment, there was a frantic verbal exchange between driver and co-pilot to agree on the best spot to cross over to the commune on the other side. And because of the incoming traffic, we would only get one chance to cross over to the hills. The darkness of the northern urban perimeter looked like the very edge of the world.

"Mummy, are we really about to cross over to the other side?"

This time, mother had no answer. She just held me tightly in her arms. Revving up the engine, the driver slammed down the accelerator and sped across the width of the motorway. Without slowing, he sent the vehicle up the gravelly mound.

I shut my eyes tight and for a moment felt like we were riding the crest of a very big wave as the momentum carried the vehicle up the slope before hurtling down over the railway tracks with a loud crunch. In a matter of seconds, we had left behind the most notorious neighbourhood of the city and ventured into the most unknown and forgotten sector.

Once the car had stabilised sufficiently, it wound its way along an uneven makeshift road, creaking under our weight and brushing against bushes and shrubs. The engine groaned with extra strain as we made a tortuous ascent up a mountainside and along a steep, narrow slope. I continued to cling tightly to my mother's hand.

Through the car's headlights, we caught our first glimpse of a series of ramshackle houses spread messily over the side of the hill separating Santa Marta's outer limits from the fishing village of Taganga on the other side of the mountain range. We passed row after row of makeshift dwellings mostly built of mouldy corrugated zinc sheets. The dim light of kerosene lamps flickered through their small windows.

Finally, the taxi came to a stop on a flat stretch of land near the top of the hill where a cluster of less than a dozen houses stood on precarious foundations. These, the outcome of displaced communities, were known as 'invasions'. Beside them stood a comparatively spacious dwelling where we would apparently be spending the next few days.

Asking us to stay in the car, Natalia walked up a slope to the entrance and knocked on the door in what sounded like a code. The door opened discreetly and a brief conversation ensued with an occupant in the shadows. Natalia then proceeded to help mum take our suitcase from the trunk of the vehicle under the moonlight. A man opened the front door for us and quietly bid us welcome.

The first room in the house was a small triangular lounge, in which a flickering lamp cast its light on a large, unframed print of the Sacred Heart stuck to the wall, whose eyes seemed to follow us around the place. On the left side of the space, an arch like entrance gave onto an inner room concealed by a curtain. On the right, another curtain gave access to a corridor that led to two private rooms, one of which had been assigned to us. We were ushered into a small bedroom that reeked of insecticide, with two beds that filled most of the space and a single window covered by a perforated nylon mesh. The brick walls that did not quite reach the ceiling were lit by the dancing flame of a lonely candle resting on a bedside table, overflowing with an accumulation of solidified paraffin from dozens of other candles that had melted on its surface.

The heat in there was horrendous. Natalia showed up with a beaten-up aluminium jug of warm water that mum and I gulped down in a matter of seconds. Sitting on the edge one of the beds, I watched the two women talking quietly while unpacking our luggage. Natalia was apologising profusely over her previous choice of "safe house".

I endeavoured to process the events of the last few days, but felt so exhausted that I closed my eyes and immediately surrendered to a deep sleep. In a recurring dream, I watched mum repeatedly assuming the role of a tireless goalkeeper struggling to keep the ball from hitting the back of the net in a never-ending game of football.

I was suddenly awakened by the sharp sound of mosquitoes buzzing around my head and noticed the candle next to the bed was out. A beam of silvery moonlight sneaked through the small window, as mum and Natalia continued to talk quietly. I asked to be shown to the bathroom as I had no knowledge of the house.

Natalia and I silently crossed the triangular room by the light of a lamp beneath a large depiction of Christ on the wall who appeared to be observing every step we took. She held me by the hand, parting the curtain as we entered the darkness of a large room where the air was heavy and stagnant and from where we could glimpse the doorless exit to an outside patio. Guided by the nocturnal glow from the back yard outside, we walked silently across the room. As my eyes became accustomed to the dark, I spotted the surreal sight of a half-open human hand on the floor. Suddenly wide awake, I then identified an inert pair of arms and feet in the half light. As I scanned the floor around us, an alarming assortment of more human limbs appeared all around. Numerous bunk beds full of bodies became visible on both sides, stacked up against the walls. With my heart pounding in my ears, I scampered out of the vast room leaving Natalia behind, until I finally emerged hyperventilating into the crisp night air outside.

The bathroom in the small patio was a tiny enclosure consisting of three sheets of zinc without a roof and a leaky hose pipe on a stone pan as the main source of running water. Next to it was a large aluminium cylinder filled to the brim with ice cold water with a floating calabash bowl in it. As I rinsed my hands, I looked up to the vastness of the sky and beheld a clear night full of stars that appeared to be much closer than ever.

"Four dockers... six winchers... five silo operators... three drivers... seven conductors..."

The lexicon of maritime tasks from the early morning broadcast on a distant radio was loud enough to wake me from a deep sleep. As far as I was concerned, it was still the middle of the night, since I could barely make out mum's silhouette in the other bed. According to the radio, it was four in the morning and all the reanimated dock workers in the spooky large room who not long ago appeared dead to the world were currently fortifying themselves with cups of strong black coffee and salt bread, courtesy of the owner of the place. The men all had swarthy complexions from endless hours toiling under the sun. The owner of the place, a burly gent with trimmed curled hair and white beard, approached us and poured milk into our coffee. In the presence of strangers, my behaviour either ranged from withdrawn to self-absorbed, or I ended up asking so many questions that I became the very definition of unbearable. Determined to bond, and possibly because of all the caffeine, I approached a group of strangers sitting around a table and began to ask what life was like in the 'terminal', as everybody used to call the seaport. I also insisted on knowing whether the fabled yellow train from Zona Bananera, immortalised in song, actually carried all the bananas that were sold around the world.

87

The house on top of the hill was a resting place for seasonal workers earning a living in the nearby maritime port. The seaport itself consisted of half a dozen docks where experienced personnel distributed shipping containers carrying liquid and general cargo, as well as sorting coal freight that reached the port daily by rail. Aware of how relatively close we were to the railway line, my abiding wish was to witness the train arriving under its own steam as it entered the city. While I was going on about that, and probably trying everyone's patience, the lights of an approaching vehicle flickered into the room through a window, whereupon the entire team of dock workers stood up and, as if one, began filing out of the house. The creaking noise of the engine of a large distribution truck featuring the Postobon soft-drink company logo emblazoned on each side became louder and louder, until the high tonnage transportation came to a shuddering stop in front of the house. One by one, the men jumped onto the back of the truck like trained cadets before disappearing downhill along the dark and dusty road.

I returned to bed, as my asthma symptoms had come back with a vengeance. While waiting for the sun to come up, I spent a few contemplative minutes loosening my last remaining milk tooth with the tip of my tongue.

At noon, frustrated by not being allowed to explore the surroundings of the hill by myself, let alone catch a glimpse of the train, I sat on the edge of a corner of the house taking in the majesty of the scenic landscape, on a cloudless sunny day that exuded calm and solitude. My vantage point afforded a panoramic view of the city's historic city centre and the gridded streets of Pescaíto where the old salt mines used to be, and I finally understood why the city of Santa Marta was called 'The Pearl of America', facing the blue waters of the Atlantic from the bottom of a valley descending all the way to the sea from Sierra Nevada, the tallest maritime mountain in the world. The old town originally populated by the Betoma people had been known as Saturna by its indigenous inhabitants before its appropriation by the Spanish crown. Today, as I watched from the summit, the city below looked tiny, dwarfed by the immensity of the Caribbean Sea, its guardian El Morro now no bigger than a pebble in the ocean.

To my right, the makeshift road that provided the only access from the outside world to the commune loomed like an antediluvian toboggan scarred by grooves of erosion, its winding path vanishing from view among thorny bushes and clusters of cacti. The small commune was supplied by weekly provisions that included perishables and cooking-gas cylinders, all of which arrived at irregular intervals on the back of a donkey. The meagre population of the commune was mostly made up of hardworking first and second generation settlers who, despite lacking electricity and running water, had made the most of life as it was.

Mother and Natalia had ventured down the hillside in search of one of the few houses that had a telephone connection, giving me the opportunity to be alone with my thoughts. While I waited for their return, strains of accordion music, the distinctive sound of *vallenato*, got louder and louder as the owner of the house emerged with a transistor in his hand and sat beside me. It was then that I first noticed the man only had one arm.

"Enjoying the view?"

I nodded silently.

"I have travelled to the other side of the world and there is no other city anywhere quite like it", the man observed nostalgically, as the first verse of a song called *El Almirante Padilla* sounded its poetic cautionary tale of a drug trafficker getting his comeuppance at the hands of the authorities.

"You hear the name in that song? Admiral José Prudencio Padilla... he was a real person... He kept the Spanish invaders off our beaches during the War of Independence two hundred years ago. That beautiful city glowing like a pearl down below owes Admiral Padilla an immense debt of gratitude", he said solemnly with a smile, before adding wryly "Instead, they named a police gunboat after him". With an air of resignation he added "And, unfortunately for the Admiral, he then backed the wrong horse, going to fight alongside Napoleon in Trafalgar, was captured and ended up scrubbing warships somewhere in England."

"What happened to your arm?" I asked with interest as I looked at the stump below his left shoulder. Exhaling wistfully, he took a few moments before I heard him speak again: "I went to war myself, son. Got my arm blown off in an explosion."

I winced visibly, picturing the incident with difficulty.

"Me and many fellow Colombians were conscripted by the UN. To 'keep the peace', they said. Instead, we were sent to fight in Korea, a land I'd never even heard of... 163 of us never came back. I was one of the lucky ones... a few of us are now just about surviving on this hill without a pension" his voice trailed off as he petted a flea-ridden skinny white dog that had approached us.

"Just like our forgotten town up here in the mountains, that conflict came to be known as 'The Forgotten War'. Three million people died in action". He frowned. "And there was a higher civilian death toll than in War World Two and Vietnam put together…" the man uttered sombrely as he stared at the immensity of the sky. "Worst 'police action' ever… No peace treaty was ever signed, so, unlike Vietnam, there's probably still a war raging somewhere over there…"

Before the man had finished speaking, the voices of mother and Natalia were calling out to us from below. We both turned to see them climbing the side of the hill from a cluster of huts below, carrying provisions they had managed to buy from the rider of the delivery donkey.

During the conversation that started while mum was boiling a bunch of green bananas for us all, I realised the previous hour or two had been given to making alternative accommodation arrangements on the phone. There had also been unwelcome developments. The taxi used the previous night to transport us to the commune had sustained extensive mechanical failure following the driver's attempt to exit the hill and now lay out of commission in a car repair shop somewhere in town, which would severely restrict our ability to get into and around the city. It was only then that I learned mum had sold our family vehicle to someone in Barranquilla some weeks ago, a beige-and-blue Chevrolet Bel Air 56 that she estimated would have been too easy to identify if seen driving around the city. For now, the income from the sale of that car was enabling her to cover our transport and living expenses. Most alarmingly, however, a telephone conversation had yielded news of a police raid on the hostel we had hastily abandoned just a few minutes earlier the night before, all of which served to confirm the women's worst fears that F-2 informants had been hard at work in the red-light district, eager to pinpoint our location.

After we all had finished wolfing down dollops of green banana purée under the all-seeing Sacred Heart on the wall, the four of us sat on metal rocking-chairs outside the house to enjoy the mountain air before the midday sun got too vicious. Somewhere in our vicinity, the ubiquitous radio struggled to transmit an audible signal due to the high altitude and I passed the time trying to ignore the adult small talk around me whilst keeping the flies off the sleepy, emaciated neighbourhood dog that had decided to keep us company, and whom I decided to call "Joe", after the dog in *Run, Joe, Run*, a popular Saturday morning television series of the day.

The ex-serviceman pointed at his clapped-out radio and I began to believe there was always a place for moribund radio transistors everywhere we went. The burly, heavily-built man who had earlier introduced himself as

Esteban, addressed my mum directly, his prematurely aged features looking haggard and harsh in the cold light of day: "The neighbours and I sat gathered around this very radio the morning you gave that interview. It took some balls to do what you did but somebody needed to say it publicly."

For a few seconds there was an awkward silence, long enough for me to observe the uncomfortable body language of the three adults, and I got the curious sense that I was in the way.

"I guarantee you and your boy will be safe in this commune for as long as you wish to stay. Nobody can approach these hills without our knowing." Looking at Natalia, Esteban's voice then began to break in the same way as when he had reminisced on the fate that had befallen his colleagues on the other side of the world some twenty years back. "Natalia has been telling us a lot about you. And I'm grateful for everything you did for her when she was alone in that prison cell. All the women on the north side of town are now living in fear. We're hearing more and more of our girls are being thrown into those hell holes… Several of them have not been heard from again."

"I'm afraid it runs far deeper than that" mum gave a guarded response, very much aware of my presence. "I just hope I get the chance to uncover some more … but it's getting complicated."

I knew very little about my mother's job and she was never one to expand on the nature of her work. All I knew was that she had served in both the army and the police and, in my simplistic binary way of perceiving life through a prism of primary colours, like those on the unblemished uniform of my paper toy soldiers, her public service was life-affirming proof to me that she could only be one of the good guys.

Keeping a cautious eye on me as if she could read my thoughts, mum ran her fingers gently through my hair and continued her coded conversation as though describing the progress of a board game. "We are keeping one step ahead of them for now, but I've been among them for long enough to know they have a sophisticated network of snitches across the suburbs. And believe me, it won't be long before they find us. Which is why, for everyone's sake, we need to leave this area as soon as possible."

The following morning looked and felt exactly like the previous one, dark and cold, heralded as usual by the crackle of the battered radio announcing the maritime terminal's vacancies for the working day ahead in drone-like bursts. Our luggage lay already packed on mum's bed, ready to be loaded onto the same truck that would be taking the team of workers to the seaport. Once again, I looked up at the fading blackness of a sky still adorned with constellations of stars. Taking a deep breath, I grabbed the calabash bowl and poured the icy water from the aluminium tank over my head.

I had barely finished tying the laces of my trainers when the incoming lights of the soda truck filtered through the window, coming to an abrupt stop in front of the house. We bid hasty goodbyes to both Esteban and Natalia and, for one last time, I watched as a group of over fifteen dockers got on the back of the truck. This time it was also our turn to join the others in the vehicle and, thrillingly enough, mom and I would be sitting in the passenger seat alongside the driver, a thin man with tamarind-coloured skin in a cap who must have driven up and down the course of the hills of San Martín so often he could likely achieve the feat blindfolded. Having turned the heavy vehicle around, he stepped on the accelerator sending it careening down the mountainous slide that passed for a road, the headlights illuminating the uneven stony terrain while the unperturbed workers at the back could be heard merrily singing the chorus of a *vallenato* song at the top of their voices.

Like a recurring dream, a swarm of butterflies fluttered anxiously in my belly as we gained speed over treacherous potholes that made the fragile chassis reverberate with a shuddering tremor, kicking up dust inside the cabin and making it difficult to breathe. I felt mum cling to me with her arms around my waist while I grasped the dashboard to stop myself from hitting the roof or being sent through the windshield. A knot had formed in my throat by the time the truck finished its descent from the hill and, at the same speed, crossed over the railway tracks of the legendary yellow train that, as it turned out, I never did get to see.

We reentered a completely different world, continuing our journey along the newly built Via Alterna, a dual carriageway resembling an airstrip lit by a lengthy row of amber streetlights, culminating at the seaport's main entrance, where we felt revived by a brisk breeze that filled our lungs with clean sea air.

The place we got out at was the westernmost location of the old salt mines and the site of the city's first railway station, built by The Santa Marta Railway Company Limited under the auspices of the United Fruit Company, which had been responsible for the infrastructure of the entire region.

The construction of the railway and the seaport, together with the arrival of ships from Europe and the resulting program of home building, turned the northern area of the city into a worker's citadel that subsequently became the sprawling neighbourhood known today as Pescaíto – the birthplace of Colombian football. A makeshift pitch next to the maritime terminal was the spot where teams made up of local workers, English adventurers and Jamaican sailors played the country's very first game of football.

The dockers disembarked one by one, still singing loudly and playfully patting me on the head as they passed by me on their way to the anchored ships, warehouses and monumental silo towers dwarfing the docks which, from a distance, could be seen bathed in amber light. Parked not far from the main entrance was the taxi that had been ordered in advance to pick us up. The new driver, who was yet another unfamiliar face to get used to, helped with our suitcase while mum looked distracted, as though entranced by the surrounding scenery, the morning light infusing the setting with an otherworldly glow. Her eyes fixed on a particular spot between the seafront and the promenade.

"This is the spot", I heard her say quietly to herself. "This is where it all began, right here."

I immediately started thinking about Georgiana and once again wondered what had become of her – whether she had managed to settle back in the green land of her native England, and whether she had kept fond memories of us despite her strange adventure when we all lived together under the same roof.

I snapped back to the present. Mum was looking in my direction, perhaps coming to realise she had let out far more than she had intended. She said nothing further as she surrounded me with her arms to the sound of crashing waves, with the urgency of someone who just wanted to hang on to what she still had. For a while, we both stood there, silent and motionless like a moment frozen in time. In the distance, the lighthouse blinked intermittently and in the middle of the ocean El Morro reflected the pastel coloured light of a brand new day.

CHAPTER 16

Old Friends

Late September, 1977

I never knew how long the journey was to get to 20 de Julio, a commune of hastily built brick dwellings in a grid of unpaved streets. I woke up the moment the engine was turned off and the sun's rays shone on my sleepy face, through the leaves of a *matarratón* tree in front of a small orange house. Named after the country's Independence Day, the neighbourhood was an array of disparate-looking dwellings uneasily aligned with one another. Some were made of brick and appeared mostly unfinished, others resembled shanty-town shacks, while a handful were mud huts with corrugated zinc roofs, all built on land colonised by fifteen displaced families that had gravitated from the suburbs of the north. Conspicuously located in a corner by an establishment serving alcoholic refreshments stood a legendary ancient tree everybody called La Bonga, a gargantuan landmark displaying centuries of scars, graffiti and all manner of modern-era mistreatment on its thick, bulging bark.

Hortensia Ledesma, a slim and slightly withered lady in her late sixties, emerged from her house wearing a patterned green dress. Once upon a time, her late husband had been a labourer in one of the coffee farms managed by my maternal grandfather and, despite the age gap between her and my mother, their friendship stretched back to their formative years. They hugged each other fondly and it wasn't long before they started reminiscing about the good old days. In the space of an hour, mum and I had gone from being recipients of the kindness of strangers to being welcomed with open arms.

However, in a short while mum had once again embarked on another of her endless telephone conferences, as had become something of a ritual every time she and I relocated to a new place. Defeated by fatigue, I succumbed to a deep sleep on a nearby rocking-chair, only to be called by the women to join them for a lunch of scrambled eggs, our first proper meal in days.

Sitting around a dining table in the middle of four walls of exposed brick, mum finally felt relaxed enough to remove the scarf that covered her head. She had also removed the sunglasses that up to that moment had kept her dark-brown eyes hidden from view and her face stood revealed in the intense glow from the sandy plot of land opposite the house. I was immediately struck by how emaciated she looked. Her once youthful features had deteriorated and her complexion now had a greyish tone.

I reached for mum's glasses now lying unattended on the table and put them on myself to reflect the bright sunlight. Walking over to the curtainless window to see the world outside, I marvelled at the arid landscape where a group of local boys were kicking a rubber ball about.

The women's conversation had veered to anecdotes of a far more distant past, recalling rural life in a remote coffee farm known as Transjordania and the neighbouring hacienda Jirocasaca, where from a very young age and well into her school years before qualifying as a nurse, mum had grown up working the land alongside her father, a highly regarded physician and botanist who traded medicinal remedies with the region's indigenous inhabitants. The farm, an idyllic corner of Magdalena's coffee growing epicentre, had been founded in the 1930s by a Belgian entrepreneur who had fallen in love with the mountain. Situated one thousand six hundred meters above sea level, the environs of Transjordania were a place where exotic birds roamed freely, a land that yielded all manner of tropical fruit and where its inhabitants breathed clean fresh air and drank water from crystalline springs fed by streams descending from the snowy peaks of the Sierra Nevada. All that changed in the course of the 1950s with the arrival of developers from south of the country, who in incursions not seen since the gold rush colonised much of the Sierra's habitable land. This paved the way for the later arrival of *marimberos* – a slang term for narcotraffickers – who illegally displaced the coffee cultivators in the early 1970s. Much of the arable land was then given over to the far more profitable cultivation of cannabis and coca leaves, adversely transforming the ecosystem and forever altering the character and functioning of the region.

It filled me with joy that even in the middle of our peripatetic existence mum was still able to find some momentary respite reminiscing about old times with an old friend from her early life. What was more endearing was discovering that Hortensia held mum in such high esteem that she had named one of her own daughters after her. They also broached the subject of the imminent start of my secondary school term, before the conversation turned to mum's infamous radio interview, which everyone we had met so far on our journey appeared to have paid particular attention to. I glanced around the room, just in case a radio transistor happened to be part of the setting and, sure enough, I soon spotted a vintage radio sitting on a cupboard.

Suddenly I heard the small roar of an engine approaching and noticed a small cloud of dust on the horizon. Within seconds, a motorbike had come to a stop outside the house and I immediately recognised Natalia as she got off the back seat. She brought in a plastic bag of groceries, including a quite revolting cod liver oil emulsion which I had been made to take since I was a toddler owing to chronic pneumonia, and other pharmaceutical products which mum had trotted off a list in her earlier telephone marathon. Mother had been suffering from insomnia, doubtless as a result of worrying that my episodes of asthma and inflammation had taken a turn for the worse. Natalia wore a brand new cap with the Union Magdalena football club logo emblazoned on the front, which she removed upon entering the house. It had not escaped my attention that no matter how mundane the situation, she always appeared to walk to the sound of imaginary cumbia drums and with the cadence of someone who had been born with rhythm in her blood. She looked at me and placed the cap upon my head, getting close enough for me to smell a strangely alluring mixture of perfume and laundry detergent.

"Migue, I want you to wear this. It will protect you from the sun. I know it's not much but I want you to know you are very much in my thoughts and hope you get better".

While mum and Natalia convened in the kitchen to exchange words in private, I sat at a dining table adorned by a purple vase of artificial flowers. I was joined by Hortensia, who now looked at me with her sad glaucous eyes that had probably seen it all in this life.

"Child", she said to me in a low voice whilst pointing at my mum, "your mother is a survivor."

This term was familiar to me and immediately brought to mind the anecdote of mother as a young girl surviving the potentially fatal bite of a coral snake near the Transjordania hacienda a lifetime away, and it was likely Hortensia herself had witnessed the event.

"Above all", she continued, now pointing to the radio on her cupboard "she has proven herself a woman of integrity...", nodding her head with each syllable. "And you, young man, you must persevere to live up to that... sacrifice... not just for yourself but for the benefit of everybody."

Noting my bewilderment, she continued her counsel carefully, choosing her words, blinking with palpable urgency and simplifying everything down to the barest essentials.

"Therefore, yes, study as much as you can. This is what we as parents traditionally expect our children to do… but, far more important than a formal education… above everything else… strive to always do the right thing by everybody, no matter the consequences. Hopefully, in a not too distant future after you have spread your wings – and that day will come much sooner than you think – we may all finally find comfort in having upright individuals doing what is right for the common good."

Then, directing a wistful gaze towards the kitchen where mum appeared to be engaged in last minute negotiations with Natalia, the old lady exhaled. "I just hope she herself may find some comfort in life at the end of it all…"

That night mum and I shared a single bed covered by a mosquito net that failed to prevent us from getting bitten throughout the night. Mother had noticed with alarm that I had developed a compulsion for going to bed with a spoonful of sugar in my mouth, to wipe the foul aftertaste of my nightly dose of cod liver oil, and I had been duly reprehended for it. The room was next to a small yard in which there was a brick shower cubicle whose tank dripped continuously throughout the night, the sound competing with the chirping sound of crickets in the mango trees. My eyesight had grown used to the darkness and I could see swarms of mosquitoes above our heads but fought off the temptation to swat them as mum seemed to be in a deep sleep.

That was the moment I heard her voice: "Please forgive me. I was not able to secure a place for you at San Luis Beltrán. I know how much you wanted a place there but I just could not afford to pay for the school term."

Mother's word had always been her bond. On the rare occasions when she apologised so categorically for something, it was an indication that she had exhausted every available avenue. Ever since my return from Bogotá, it had been evident that mother was having to manage in unprecedented financial difficulties. The road disrepair problem kept her from running her business on the farm, our house now had to be leased to tenants, plus there was matter of the sale of her car and the repair bills for one of her taxis, all of which amounted to an absolute reversal of fortune on every front. Therefore, the news that I would not be starting my baccalaureate in my chosen school did not altogether come as a surprise. Still, the notion that I would not be joining any of my primary school friends in the next stage of our education made me bite my lips in frustration and felt about as welcome as a blow to the stomach.

"Mum, the lady of the house advised me to study a lot, to get ahead in life, … but she also told me that doing the right thing by everybody is far more important… So, I promise that, from this moment on, I will always strive to do the right thing, only because I want you to be proud of me."

There was a brief lull before mum's words could be heard again: "I'm already proud of you, my son. Don't do it because of me."

She allowed herself a faint chuckle as she finished her sentence. "Besides, I know it's in your nature to want to do what is right."

I was already having to compete with the piercing buzzing of the mosquitoes swarming within the protective environment of the mosquito net. Irritated by the disruption, I sat up on the edge of the bed intent on eradicating as many of them as possible by clapping my hands all around.

"But please do not be afraid if things get more than a little bumpy before they get better", mum continued while I debated on bringing some water for us from the kitchen as my throat was feeling parched from thirst.

"Is there anything you want me to do for you, mummy?"

Before her response came, I looked in astonishment at the palms of my hands where a mixture of dead mosquitoes and the sticky crimson of our intermingled bloods had become visible in the half light.

"Yes my love. Above all, I need you to be strong."

CHAPTER 17

The Corner of Joy

Early October, 1977

The previous week, a meeting had been arranged with mother's lawyer, Marco Vinicio Suárez, at a drinking establishment near the home of her friend Rosa Herrero, a boisterous and charismatic *mulata* in her fifties who had agreed to take us in as temporary guests in her house.

The house where we were to spend the next few days, where Rosa lived with her husband and four children, had been one of the first dwellings built by the territorial credit institute for victims of the community of Bastidas, after she and her family were rendered homeless when the river there burst its banks. Their replacement property was a house embedded on a steep hill, which could only be accessed by a long row of cement steps.

The driver put our suitcase in the back of the taxi before starting the engine, we hugged Hortensia goodbye and she watched us from her all-seeing window as we quietly vacated her premises under a cloudy afternoon. We were whisked away to Bastidas, the easternmost suburb widely acknowledged for its festive atmosphere and whose community life revolved around a conspicuous white church in the middle of a spacious and lively main square where a third of all the premises consisted of drinking taverns and fast food outlets.

"Doña, may I just say you can rely on me to be on call anytime you need a driver or anything delivered", offered the driver as he drove us past the church. Mother was having difficulty paying her few remaining workers' wages and dreaded the day when she no longer had any drivers in her employ, which is why the following words she heard must have come as a huge relief:

"My wife and I heard you on the radio and we have deep, deep admiration for you. Don't hesitate to leave a message with her if I'm out and about". He pulled the car up in front of a spot known as The Corner of Joy, a lively tavern popular with seasoned card and domino players who passed the time to the sound of boleros from yesteryear.

Rosa, a broad and charismatic lady widely regarded as the life and soul of the party, was in the process of greeting guests arriving at the establishment when she saw us emerge from the taxi. She welcomed us with energetic hugs and a resounding laugh. She and my mother had had a long-standing friendship since their days at Licorera Del Magdalena, a liquor factory where mum had held a position as auditor in the comptroller's office prior to her stint in the army at the Cordova Infantry Battalion. The main event scheduled at the venue that evening was the imminent return of Rosa's youngest son from completing his military service.

As we entered the place we were greeted by the sound of melancholy Mexican boleros, courtesy of a counterfeit Wurlitzer under blinking ceiling lights around which a myriad moths and butterflies fluttered incessantly. One wall of the room was decorated with framed portraits of different iterations of the Unión Magdalena football team alongside old maps featuring Colombia when Panama was still part of the country. The barman, a jolly middle-aged chap, immediately offered to make me an oatmeal shake "on the house".

Mother and I sat at one of the tables against the back wall of the place where we were eventually joined by Marco Vinicio, who for as long as I could remember ruffled my hair every time he saw me and was fond of addressing me as 'champ'. A bespectacled man in his early sixties, informally attired in one of his customary guayabera shirts, he approached our table from the bar carrying a tray with the promised humongous glass of oat shake for me and beers for mum and himself. At the other end of the room Rosa could be seen chatting to the guests as she distributed yet another freshly prepared round of *empanadas* for those gathered in expectation of her son's homecoming. Her energetic banter and merciless admonishment of her husband and his card-playing buddies could clearly be heard from a distance. Through the cacophonous din swirling around us, Marco Vinicio brought mother up to speed on recent developments.

"On the one hand, your financial situation continues to be precarious. On the other, there are some welcome developments concerning other matters I've been mediating on your behalf. Your application for the management of a small retail business in the city has been approved by a textile company based in Medellín. The obvious advantage with this position is there won't be any need for you to be present at the retail premises on a daily basis."

Taking a giant gulp from my big glass and despite not yet having a head for finances, I wondered if these glad tidings represented some light at the end of the tunnel for mum, who of late appeared to be struggling even to retain the service of the two taxi drivers that remained in her employ.

Two more beers arrived and the empty glasses soon accumulated around the table. By then, the conversation between mum and her lawyer, which was now revolving around home rentals and possible transfers or sales of properties, had attained the distinct patina of 'adult talk', much of it unintelligible to my ears and soon causing me to tune out as usual. Mother then produced a thick bundle of official-looking documents from her purse and requested Marco Vinicio make photocopies for her file. Crossing my arms, and beginning to find the noise around me somewhat monotonous and distracting, I sat back and gave myself over to observing swarms of moths fluttering around the ceiling lights, as if some invisible force was preventing them from breaking free from their circular trajectory.

It was then that Marco Vinicio alluded to 'movements' and to 'walls having ears'. In the codified language of the adult world metaphors are often loaded with meaning. Furthermore, and irrespective of context, phrases such as 'don't let your guard down' and 'they are forcing you into retreat', are bound to sound ominous and dark to the uninitiated. Perhaps I had been too ensconced in my own enclave of safety to join up any of the dots connecting the thread of the ongoing conversation. Pursuing the inverse maxim that adults were better heard and not seen, I began to pay attention, briefly wondering why windows, or even tables in their world, should not be mentioned in the same breath as other inanimate objects said to be in possession of 'ears'. At that precise moment I heard somebody uttering "Your move!" in our vicinity. My attention immediately switched to the neighbouring table on the right and my eyes locked on a chessboard between two players facing one another in intense concentration.

"For now, we may very well be one step ahead of them", Marco Vinicio continued, as mum listened intently in her corner. "But now's not the time to be complacent. My guess is their strategy is to carry on checking every nook and cranny while they wait for you to make the wrong move."

I pondered on the first and last time I had heard the word 'strategy', fully conscious of its meaning, while keeping an eye on the adjacent table where the chess players seemed to have reached a stalemate. With bizarre symmetry, the Queen was cornered by a combination of bishops and knights, with no apparent means available for her to make her escape and, for a moment, the lawyer's words closely mirrored the state of play on the chessboard, endowing the game with an unexpected theatricality.

"Let's face it. You were an anomaly to them from the very beginning. A woman in a male-dominated environment unexpectedly taking matters into her own hands and risking everything. A single mother with a minor to look after, no less. In other words, someone with a lot to lose."

Recalling Francesca's chess lessons in my school library, the Queen always acts of her own accord and without the direction of the King. However, she depends on the loyalty of her friendly pieces if cornered. I thought of Natalia and Esteban, as well as of half a dozen other people who had provided assistance and given us shelter over the past few days. I then cast my eyes back at the chessboard on the neighbouring table just in time to see the Queen narrowly outmanoeuvring the opposing knight by effecting the only possible movement available to her.

"No matter how much you move, you can no longer ignore the risk", Marco Vinicio continued. Unlike the King, the Queen has a multitude of movements at her disposal but she cannot jump over other pieces. And if she were to move in a straight line, her path would be blocked by either friends or foes. The Queen I was now watching did not appear to have any options left, except one: there was a strategy that involved the loss of the Queen in order to achieve victory in the game. According to what I remember from my time spent at the school library with Tamara, this was known as 'The Queen's Sacrifice'.

I never got to know how the game at the next table ended. Needing some fresh air, I headed for the exit with visions in my head of a colossal chessboard that stretched all the way from the hills of San Martín to the outer limits of the northern suburbs.

Leaving the gaming tables behind me and walking by Rosa's family members and groups of her friends from the neighbourhood gathered at the entrance of the tavern waiting to welcome her son, I squeezed my way out of the premises just in time to be dazzled by the dying rays of a setting sun infusing the main square with golden tones. My senses were immediately assaulted by the bustling street ambience as I dodged incoming street revellers now beginning to grow in number. A speeding vehicle sounded its horn, its driver shouting an expletive in my direction and narrowly missing me as I crossed the wide unpaved road absentmindedly, as though endowed with a protective force field. Finding an empty space on the pavement on the other side of the road, I sat on the edge of the square under the shadow of the San Judas Tadeo parish church and immersed myself in my thoughts until the sun had completely disappeared from view.

Not far from where I was, a street vendor of flavoured *granizados* pushing his wares gradually along the pavement approached me as I was in the grip of another one of my panic attacks, the noise from the wheels of his cart making a screeching sound as he came to a stop by my side.

"Are you lost, lad? Where do you come from?"

I raised my head and saw an unshaven, partially toothed, thin man in his forties looking me over. His eyes were fixed on my shirt, shorts and my sneakers, a big brand sportswear. "You're definitely not from around here. Could it be your mom is looking for you?"

By now, I wished I had a penny for every time a stranger asked me about my mum and, for a second, I revelled in my "originality". That was the moment a lengthy convoy of large merchandise vehicles arrived in procession along the main road looking like a celebration parade, transporting monolithic custom-made sound speakers on their cargo beds. The legendary *'picós'* – derived from the English 'pick-up' – were monumental pieces of equipment designed to liven up large street festivities. A constant feature on carnival floats, some stood well over six feet high and were decorated with painted scenes in vibrant colours emblazoned with names such as 'El Último Hit', 'El Sonoro' or 'El Destroyer', and whose explosive bottom range felt like being struck in the middle of your chest. Once the parade of trucks had thinned out from view leaving my ears ringing, I saw the figure of a tall, lanky middle-aged, moustachioed man dressed in festive colourful apparel approaching me directly from across the street. I immediately recognised him as Heraclio Rodríguez, Rosa's husband, who along with other family members had been busy trying to find my whereabouts for the past ten minutes.

"My boy, don't do stuff like that, your mum is having a nervous breakdown back there thinking you've been kidnapped or something!"

Full of remorse and blushing like a beetroot, I followed Heraclio back to the tavern and was astounded by the pitiful sight of mum and her lawyer standing by the entrance, both looking aghast and absolutely petrified over my sudden disappearance. Rushing to me immediately, before Heraclio and I had even finished crossing the road, mum grabbed me by the shoulders and whispered in my ear: "Please don't do this to me again".

The attention of the people who had gathered around us was suddenly diverted by the arrival of Rosa's son, who had been brought in the back of a beat-up Chevrolet. He beamed a broad, pearly smile to all and sundry as he stepped off, arms outstretched, in his green-and-brown army uniform and black cadet boots. Meanwhile, on the corner of the street, mum held me in a firm and long embrace that lasted long after the last languid notes of a melancholic bolero from the canteen's Wurlitzer had finished playing.

CHAPTER 18

El Liceo

An instrumental version of the traditional old song *El Pescador de mi Tierra* that always introduced a morning radio program popular with early risers blared from a ramshackle transistor radio that someone had turned on in the kitchen. We had spent our first night in Bastidas and, as was becoming the norm, I was awake before sunrise. No matter how often it happened, I was unable to get the hang of waking up in a different house every time I opened my eyes first thing in the morning. I could barely remember the events of the night before, nor the long climb with our suitcase all the way up the steep stairs that led to Rosa's house. The pain in my limbs, however, was all too real.

The family bustle and the oily smell of freshly made *empanadas* caused me to rise and jump out of the lower part of a bunk bed I had shared with mum that night. The electricity supply all over the suburb was out but that had not stopped Rosa from making *empanadas* and fresh coffee with firewood, the smoke from the kitchen escaping in an upward stream through the small patio window while she energetically fanned the embers with a piece of cardboard – which in many ways reminded me of grandma's resourcefulness and can-do spirit when she always made sure supper was ready for a whole contingent of people back at the big yellow house. Despite the comical nature of the moment and the bonhomie between mum and the others so early in the morning, an all-pervading heaviness hung in the air. As a consequence, the house appeared to be much older than it actually was, its colourful walls already showing signs of subsidence and hairline cracks were already in evidence on its concrete kitchen floor.

Mid October, 1977

Today was a key day for me because, in a matter of hours, I would be enrolling in the Instituto de San Sebastián de Urabá for the start of my secondary school term in three month's time. Despite my nerves, I was looking forward to what I considered to be a momentous stage in my life with new classmates and a new school environment. When I stepped into the dining room, I spotted everybody in the house including mum sitting around a large table, all attentively listening to Nelson, who was wearing a red-and-blue Union Magdalena T-shirt, gleefully recounting more of his exciting adventures as an army recruit in the infantry battalion off the Pacific coast, following the pivotal moment during a night out when he was unceremoniously thrown into the back of a military truck and drafted into the army.

Along with Nelson, the men in the house had all served in the army, as if it were a family tradition. At first glance, Nelson was like a younger facsimile of his father, a tall, wiry mulatto with straight hair, a consummate storyteller with a seemingly inexhaustible well of entertaining anecdotes and the natural ability to effortlessly command the attention of a roomful of people, his rapid verbal delivery coupled with lightning-fast gestures.

While everyone was distracted by tales of parachuting and the assembling and disassembling of military weaponry, I walked to the patio unnoticed and bathed quickly with cold water overflowing from another regulation aluminium cylinder that apparently everybody in the northern suburbs used for their ablutions. As I poured water over my head with a calabash bowl, only the voices of the women could be heard, staccato fragments of their conversation barely reaching my ears which alluded to mum's occupational hazards as an active member of the police force, though it was not immediately clear what any of it was connected to. Wrapped in just a towel, I rushed to the bedroom and opened the suitcase containing our possessions. I came across the paper Peter Pan which I had given my mum and which she had attempted to preserve as carefully as possible within one of the compartments. Pulling out the effigy, fragments of green felt paper that I had painstakingly cut to resemble leaves of the forest came unstuck and lay scattered all over our bed, a shattered memento of our adventures together and a redundant vestige of my childhood.

I put on a pair of beige trousers, brand new black shoes, and a plain, short-sleeved white shirt complete with black tie, a sartorial combo mum had discreetly relegated to a compartment of our luggage, intended as a gift for me for my ninth birthday. She appeared from the dining area to punch extra holes in my belt and make sure my tie was on straight. I then dutifully combed my hair in front of a mirror, hoping the mosquito bites around my face and neck were not going to be too noticeable during my interview. Shortly after, I was tucking into half a dozen *empanadas* at the table, washing them down with milk as I listened to the women taking a trip down memory lane. Rosa was a rural woman, gregarious and direct and completely devoid of the airs and graces so characteristic of mum's business associates whom Rosa now openly referred to as 'fair-weather friends'. Inevitably, the conversation turned to our ongoing quest to find accommodation. Those who knew mum acknowledged her resilience and tenacity in pulling herself up by her bootstraps. The fact that she was a single mother who simultaneously ran two moderately successful businesses while keeping a full-time position as a civil servant was still considered a rare feat in an almost exclusively male-dominated society. However, it was evident that circumstances had changed quite dramatically, forcing her to make decisions I was still struggling to understand. It was then I learned, not without dismay, that she had put the farm up for sale and was subsisting exclusively on the income generated by the rent of our family house.

When the time came for me to experience the reality of enrolling in my new school, mum and I bid Rosa goodbye and from the front door of the house spotted Heraclio, seeming animated, like a hummingbird, at the bottom of the hillside. From where we were above he looked tiny, singing loudly as he enthusiastically polished his pride and joy, a large, immaculate, custom-sprayed silver Dodge Dart, a legacy from his days as a member of the taxi drivers' guild in Santa Marta's public market square.

At exactly eight o'clock, mum and I got out of the silver car right in front of the institute, a quadrangular, austere Republic-period building painted with a powdery pollen-yellow carbide paint that, once attached to any clothing fabric, was almost impossible to remove. The building consisted of two floors and two inner courtyards that included a small football pitch without any turf. Its main façade faced a huge plot of undeveloped land that adjoined the city's public market. Students accessed the building through a side entrance leading to an atrium that reflected enough sunlight from its concrete floor to light a series of dark classrooms around it.

The interview with Rector Manuel Lemaitre Carvajal turned out to be more intimidating than I had anticipated. The rector was an imposing and improbably tall man from La Guajira with flinty rugged features that looked like they could have been chiselled on the side of a rocky mountain. A highly regarded teacher and historian who always dressed modestly but impeccably, he commanded the kind of respect usually reserved for senators and high-ranking military figures.

"Señora and Señor Monzón" he boomed in our direction with a warm smile as mother and I were ushered in. "I bid you both welcome to our school."

We seated ourselves on the other side of an enormous desk in his office, the walls of which were covered with rows of yellowed diplomas that looked as ancient as the Dead Sea scrolls.

"In our school, we pride ourselves on bringing out the very best in our students. Our goal is to make useful citizens of every young man or woman who graces our humble classrooms. We are proud to provide the very best education this country has to offer. To that end, our biology teachers are all medical professionals. For example, one of them, who happens to be my brother, is an eminently qualified surgeon. Likewise, our religious studies teacher is an actual clergyman – I myself may not believe in God but don't let that discourage you. Also, our two history teachers are published authors on a wide variety of historical subjects and the geography teachers we employ are intrepid explorers who have charted everything from the tallest mountains in the country down to the depths of our oceans. It is our belief that only enthusiastic and passionate educators who live and breathe their chosen subjects are capable of making a real difference in the classroom."

He paused to cast his eyes in the direction of the suburbs, with the resigned look of someone fully acquainted with the city and its myriad contrasts, a town that was joyous and celebratory on the surface but had shadows lurking underneath.

"Granted", he continued, "I know billiard halls and houses of ill-repute make more money than a school such as ours. But an honest and proper education is the only way we can transform society for the better."

Days turned into weeks at the *liceo* and, as groups of students congregated outdoors during school breaks to consume pieces of salted mango in the shade, it became evident that freedom from a uniform meant they could now indulge their thirst for affordable fashion in the shape of wide-lapel shirts and bell-bottomed trousers purchased from street vendors in Quinta Avenida. We had also discovered disco music, and some of the bolder ones among us perfected soaring vocal harmonies in the schoolyard of songs by the Bee Gees and Donna Summer, complete with synchronised disco dance routines.

As time went by, I was able to forge solid friendships with the majority of my peers in the classroom and we all took lectures very seriously. Among the teachers at the helm of our education that we most revered were Amilcar Daza, an eminent mathematian, Eusebio Arévalo, esteemed professor of Spanish literature and Francisco Carvajal, an imposing 6 ft 10 inch surgeon/biology teacher. From the moment he began to speak, we knew our critical thinking was going to be put to the test as never before. Not only was Francisco Carvajal a powerful public speaker but the surgical precision of his merciless cross-examinations were an effective deterrent from any idleness in the classroom, the rigour of his inquisitions invariably reducing distracted students to shameful quivering wrecks. Spurred on by this, we resolved never to enter the classroom again without a recording device, in order to keep up with Carvajal's pace, and as it turned out, there was never enough tape for his lectures, which were delivered with the strident erudition of a seasoned head of state. We made the collective decision to supplement our learning by organising a 'study club' outside school, gathering periodically in a classmate's home in the historic centre of the city so that a handful of us could carefully dissect the contents of tape recordings of lectures ranging from history to mathematics.

For her part, mum had managed to rent a semi-furnished property for us to live in, a small and unassuming two-bedroom house on a quiet street six blocks from the *liceo*. This particular development appeared to have finally put an end to the relentless instability of our peripatetic existence.

CHAPTER 19

The Marketplace

Late October, 1977

The stability of a new home had finally given me enough space to reminisce on the events of the past year, revisit notebooks with unfinished drawings and revise jottings from a diary of sorts I had kept, all of which enabled me to keep track of our ever-developing circumstances. Underlying this, though, was the sobering and often disquieting realisation that mum and I had been existing like two migrating birds constantly on the go since my return from Bogotá, which now seemed a lifetime ago.

I also felt I had at last outgrown my compulsion of wishing for 'portals' to escape from unwanted places and situations. In this new environment of relative tranquility, the frequency of my asthma attacks had significantly decreased and there was a sense that, at the end of a very strange and convoluted path, a reversal of fortune had granted mother and me a much longed-for measure of calm, as well as the hope of a future filled with endless possibilities.

Mum's income from her job as manager of a clothing store near the city centre had made it possible for her to offer Roger a contract as a regular taxi driver. His responsibilities would include maintaining in good working order one of two vehicles she still had at her disposal, and being available to collect me after school, terms he readily accepted as this would enable him to afford evening classes at the Hugo J. Bermúdez Institute for a qualification as a mechanical engineer.

Roger was talkative and cheerful, full of anecdotes and good cheer. At mum's request, he had also been tasked with taking me to my weekly 'study club', each trip to the centre of town affording me an opportunity to survey all manner of urban life through the tinted windows of the car and to become aware of buildings I had not seen before: from modern-looking dwellings from the 1950s to porticoed houses built in Republic-era style, their ornate frontages resembling cake decorations, with names such as Tomasa or Esperanza moulded on their fascias. As I watched the city's architecture in all its disparate variety open-mouthed, Roger enthusiastically extolled the virtues of classic *vallenato* versus *salsa picante*, while music from orchestras such as Fruko y sus Tesos or El Gran Combo de Puerto Rico blared out from the car speakers.

During a particularly balmy afternoon after school, we broke with our carefully arranged timetable. An uncharacteristically distracted Roger made an unscheduled stop at the marketplace to buy *empanadas* and a fizzy drink, leaving me in the car momentarily unattended.

The market square was an assault on the senses: five hundred square meters of noisy commerce teeming with scores of merchants selling products ranging from meat and dairy products and fresh seafood from local fishing villages to agricultural goods transported from farms all over the Magdalena region. Descendants of Syrian-Lebanese immigrants who a century ago had ventured on a long journey by ship to our Caribbean coasts, these merchants plied their trade and enlivened the market selling all manner of merchandise such as imported spices, multi-coloured fabrics and exotic garments.

At the centre of it all, Interstate buses built like juggernauts collected passengers from the heart of the square, leaving dark plumes of smoke in their wake. It was through this kaleidoscope of frenzied activity that I spotted an incongruous looking bookshop on a busy corner of the market, a news-stand saturated with books and with magazines leaning against one of its walls. Without thinking twice, I got out of the taxi and headed straight to the unlikely-looking retailer like a moth to a flame. I sat myself down on an empty leather chair by the entrance and began leafing through an intriguing-looking volume entitled *The Philosopher's Stone* which I had selected from a precariously balanced pile of used books. The title had brought to mind breezy evenings spent under rows of trupillo trees facing the INEM institute close to grandma's house, a meeting point where local boys from Liceo Celedón, who had taken me under their wing as something of a mascot, held lengthy brainstorming academic sessions while brandishing copies of the celebrated Cuban mathematician Baldor's Algebra book, endlessly discussing the work of Ancient Greek mathematicians and early philosophers.

At that very moment the shop owner, an obese, hirsute man from Antioquia with a wispy moustache, emerged from the cavernous interior that housed hundreds of well-thumbed second-hand tomes of every description, bringing the musty smell of ancient paper along with him.

"What the hell do you think you are doing? Sitting on my chair and browsing through my books like you own the place?"

"I'm very sorry sir, but I noticed the chair was empty and thought it was okay for me to sit here" I replied, without taking my eyes off the book, more out of embarrassment than sarcasm.

"Don't get smart with me, son!", he said, theatrically wagging a finger in my direction, even though he knew I was unlikely to run away with any of his stock. Noticing more editions of books in English, it occurred to me to ask for any literature featuring Big Ben, the Changing of the Guard or Peter Pan, all of which were synonymous with London in my mind.

"Do you have money to spend? This isn't a library … And why do I get the impression your mum must be running around like crazy looking for you?"

It was with a sense of déjà vu that I resigned myself to the idea that every unknown adult engaging with me in conversation would unfailingly end up mentioning my mother, or at least allude to her absence. Raising an eyebrow, the man looked at the book in my hands.

"I see you've picked an unusual book to pass the time."

Stroking his moustache, he then embarked on a monologue befitting an antiquarian or even a history teacher.

"Once upon a time… there was a famous library said to contain all the knowledge available to mankind. It was the great library of Alexandria. Unfortunately, all that knowledge, recorded as it was on perishable Egyptian papyrus scrolls, went up in smoke in a single night after a big fire, a lamentable event that slowed western civilisation's progress for the next five hundred years. Which just goes to show the importance of choosing incombustible material for committing important stuff to posterity!"

The monologue-come-history-lesson must have continued for several more minutes while I remained fixated on how Alexandria was the single most beautiful name I had ever heard. I quickly snapped out of my reverie when I remembered Roger, so I scrambled out of the shop to return to the taxi, without so much as bidding the dumbfounded shopkeeper a hasty goodbye.

Upon realising I had lost sight of Roger and the taxi, I was gripped by a sense of panic I had believed long relegated to the past as I squeezed my way through thick crowds of shoppers and passers-by that had seemingly materialised out of nowhere, breathing stale air saturated with the stench of raw meat being cleaved by local butchers and fishmongers. In an attempt to get away from the heaving crowd, I made for the market square, just in time to be engulfed by a giant plume of black smoke belching out from the exhaust pipe of one of the Interstate buses sounding its blaring horn as it was pulling out next to me. Seconds later, I was momentarily blinded by acrid smoke wafting accidentally into my face from the burning pan of a street cook frying *buñuelos* outdoors. Rubbing my eyes with the back of my hands, I plodded along in unfamiliar surroundings before realising I was completely lost in a nameless alleyway and, to make matters worse, due to a resumption of an asthma attack, I was struggling to get air into my lungs. The prying eyes of onlookers and the visual chaos of hand-painted colourful advertisements on the walls of continuous rows of shops and hardware stores in labyrinthine alleys saturated whatever remained of my senses with the potency of a hallucinogenic drug.

Suddenly, I felt a hand grabbing my shoulder. Through tears in my eyes, I saw Roger's face. He proceeded to scold me in a voice oscillating between furious anger and relief: "You've given me the mother of all frights! Where the hell have you been?"

"I was reading *The Philosopher's Stone*...

'*The Philosopher's Stone*?! I'll drop a stone on your thick skull if you pull another disappearing act like that, you little runt!"

Accepting Roger had a point, I decided to walk alongside him as meekly and as silently as I possibly could until we both had found our way back to the taxi. When he sternly opened the door for me, I made a feeble attempt at speaking, before being shut down by the former army recruit.

"But... but..."

"No buts! I don't want to hear anything coming out of your mouth, just get into the car before I get real mad!"

I knew I could still get in a whole heap of trouble, so I sat in the front passenger seat without further protest.

"Even so, please, please ... don't even dream of telling your mum that I lost track of you out there even for a second ... I can see her easily losing her rag over this."

With a tortuous look on his face, Roger finally realised with horror the reason I had been so apprehensive about agreeing to enter the car. Traces of fish entrails, along with other wet and smelly residues from the marketplace which had become attached to the soles of my once pristine sneakers, were now smeared in a congealed mess all over the formerly impeccable carpet in the front of mother's vehicle. I watched Roger as he banged the steering wheel with his forehead.

"Don't worry, Rog", I uttered with all the kindness I was able to muster. "Your secret is safe with me."

As it turned out, Roger's nervousness did appear to have other disquieting grounds. Having driven us both to my house, and while mother was scooping the contents of a soursop in the kitchen to make a refreshing drink for us, I ensconced myself in my room to honour my pact of silence with Roger and avoid getting him into trouble. However, I could just about make him out speaking in hushed tones in the kitchen over the intermittent din of the blender as he shared with mother news of certain recent developments in the Bastidas neighbourhood, which involved the unexpected arrival of an unfamiliar dark SUV and strangers entering the very same canteen where mother and I had met with Marco Vinicio. According to witnesses, things had been smashed by the men from the vehicle and the bartender suffered broken bones and cuts to his face, apparently for withholding information regarding the whereabouts of "wanted" newcomers that had been sighted in his establishment. Clutching a pillow as I struggled to hear the conversation from the privacy of my room, I remembered the jolly bartender who had treated me to an oatmeal shake "on the house" and then I thought about mum and the occupational hazards of being a police officer, very much hoping this alarming incident was outside her remit.

My first year at Instituto San Sebastián de Urabá concluded with an art exhibition of students' work intended to reflect our generation's priorities or preoccupations regarding the kind of society in which we saw ourselves, as the teachers in the institute encouraged students to develop a more globalised outlook on the world. One of the entries focused on the devastation that famine was still wreaking in Southern Asia, a poster-sized illustration depicting a baby, all skin and bones and crying alone and abandoned in the middle of a vast wilderness. Another was a collage of images from wartorn Vietnam, an event still fresh in people's consciousness. As for me, I remained exercised by living conditions affecting locals closer to home and resolved to make a point by producing a sculpture. Following an initial debate amongst members of the jury, my entry was disqualified from the competition for not being a poster-sized design as the rules required. It consisted of three water pipes bound together with sections of a garden hose, painted in the colours of the flag of Santa Marta, dripping with substances made from multicoloured plasticine which I had mounted on a cardboard plinth to reflect the scarcity of drinking water and the seemingly permanent overflow of raw sewage in the streets of the poorest parts of Santa Marta, something that had made an impression on me when mother and I moved from house to house in the deprived north side of the city for the best part of a year.

Mid-October, 1978

The Santa Marta Social Club had been the traditional starting point for the city's famed carnival parade since 1913. The large colonial-style compound consisted of a two-tier balconied interior overlooking a large open-air dance floor and a sound stage that for the last sixty years had been graced by the most legendary orchestras in the country. That late Wednesday afternoon the atmosphere within was sedate, the gentle sound of waves crashing on the shore outside the walls of the club competing with an endless succession of Daniel Santos boleros from a stereo sound system. Half a dozen retired legal professionals were quietly playing dominoes in one of the club's chambers when they were interrupted by the unexpected arrival of a man in his mid-thirties.

"Doctor Suárez?"

Turning to the advancing silhouette, the lawyer replied. "That would be me. And I'm certainly no doctor. Marco Vinicio Suárez, at your service".

As a law practitioner, Suárez was highly regarded in all circles of Samarian society. Unusually for a man of his profession, he was widely esteemed for his fairness and generosity, a man with the common touch who felt equally at home rubbing shoulders with members of Santa Marta's high society as playing cards with clients in some of the city's most disadvantaged neighbourhoods. Famously, he had waived his legal fees when representing local farmers who had lost their lands following twenty years of disastrous economic policies brought about by the Frente Nacional, knowing full well he was never likely to see a cent of his wages from bankrupt labourers who had lost everything, acquiring in the process a reputation for being 'a man of the people for the people'.

Producing his credentials from a pocket in his sweaty shirt, the visitor introduced himself.

"My name is Ricardo Gonzaga, from Radio Galeón. I was wondering if we could have a minute."

Excusing himself from the table, Marco Vinicio suggested heading for the nearby bar for more privacy. Ordering a beer for them both, he asked

Gonzaga about his friend and founder of Radio Galeón, Aurelio Carbonell Estrada.

"He said I was likely to find you here. I've spent the last six months trying to trace an ex-army and police officer, a lady named Carmen Monzón. I'm sure it's no coincidence, but every one of her movements has been followed by … well, let's just say the police have never been too far off her scent but she had a knack of always being two steps ahead of them. She then vanishes from the face of the earth and it's now been more than a year since anybody has had news of her whereabouts."

Feeling under scrutiny from Suárez's quizzical gaze, Gonzaga got to the point quickly.

"The boss tells me you acted as her lawyer and were actually present in the studio the day of her radio exposé … so I know I'm on the right track by coming to you."

"There are things better left unsaid", responded Suárez as he downed a glass of cold beer, "and if you expect me to divulge matters of confidentiality to a virtual stranger, then I'll tell you straight away that's just not going to happen".

"Doctor Suárez, in that case I will not insist. This is the last time you will hear me say her name."

He opened the artisan daybag on his shoulder to reassure the lawyer he was not carrying any recording equipment. "Just so you know this conversation is strictly off the record."

Gonzaga lowered his voice with each sentence, while keeping a watchful eye on the barman collecting glasses from a nearby table. "However, the girl who by most accounts had been assisting your lady client suddenly went missing more than three months ago. None of her colleagues from the north side have seen or heard from her again. It's like she's fallen off the face of the earth. Her relatives have been left fearing the worst."

The string of boleros had come to an end, leaving only the sound of the waves to break the awkward silence.

"It's taken me a while, but I have been gathering evidence of a connection between the director of the F-2 and the so called 'Birds of Prey'. Are you aware of such a link?"

"Theories connecting the two have been circulating, yes", Suárez answered, more as a means to goad the reporter to expound on the subject further. Reaching into his bag, Gonzaga produced more than a dozen Polaroid photographs with dates scribbled on them in black marker ink, which he fanned out on the bar counter like a hand of playing cards.

"See these here? I took them outside The Panamerican restaurant, turning the flash setting of the camera to avoid attracting attention to myself. But I did get close enough to capture sufficient detail. The large SUV model in this picture with the registration number you see here is the means of transport favoured by Lieutenant José Francisco Carrasco, Director of the F-2, particularly on Wednesday nights. He's a creature of habit, if there was one. And here is Carrasco again, on another Wednesday night, emerging from the same restaurant, just behind Agent Valverde, his right hand man towering over him, followed by none other than Gustavo Maldonado."

Suárez stared at the photos in silence.

"I might be overthinking this..." added Gonzaga "but, why on earth would the Director of the F-2 be meeting on a regular basis with the Mayor of Santa Marta?"

"They could just be very close friends", the lawyer dead-panned.

"Could be", responded Gonzaga. "But Carrasco's SUV is exactly the same vehicle that was used by the men who roughed up the bartender in Bastidas's 'Corner of Joy' for refusing to answer questions regarding the whereabouts of Carmen Monzón. The poor man sustained such a severe beating he's still in hospital with life-changing injuries."

"I should never have agreed to meet her in any public place", lamented Suárez ruefully through gritted teeth. "How careless and stupid of me... I have probably put everyone's safety in jeopardy without realising it."

"I promise to get to the bottom of this story if it's the last thing I do", asserted Gonzaga as he stared at the blood-red sunset fully visible from across the dancehall which for a few moments saturated the interior of the club with an unnatural luminescence. "Not a day goes by without me thinking of those mutilated bodies I saw strewn around the morgue that evening."

Appearing to snap out of a reverie, he turned to look the lawyer in the eye. "This is not the aftermath of the 'bonanza marimbera', nor is it the ongoing vendetta between the Cárdenas and Valdeblánquez clans. My instinct is we are dealing with state-sanctioned social cleansing on an industrial scale. For all we know, this gang of killers has been operating in plain sight all along."

For months, Marco Vinicio's inquisitive legal mind had conceived of that unsettling scenario being the most likely explanation and was fully certain Carmen had been justified in fleeing for her life. Unexpectedly however, he now struggled with a paradox. He was a man in his sixties, a respected pillar of the community, committed to his wife and two sons who were following in his professional footsteps by studying law in Universidad Pontificia La Javeriana in Bogotá. Widely acknowledged as a man committed to the pursuit of what was right. And yet he also knew he could never envisage wilfully exposing his family to risk of any kind, regardless of the cause. As a lawyer, he was certainly not as visible a figure as a roving reporter like Gonzaga, who was probably the same age as Carmen. However, the wedding band on the reporter's finger meant he was also a married man and probably had a family too. The troubling realisation that a man half his age standing before him was clearly intrepid enough and perhaps sufficiently haunted to make good on his promise to expose a mythical ring of executioners without apparent regard for his personal safety now niggled at his conscience.

Without showing any trace of his discomfort, he cautioned with a mixture of thrill and dread: "I would urge you to stay low while you make sure of your facts. Very sure."

CHAPTER 20

The Lost City

Mid-October, 1979

I had just turned ten the previous week. To commemorate my reaching such a milestone and emboldened by a renewed sense of calm in our lives, mother made the decision to grant me cautious permission to join a student expedition organised by our school as part of our cultural studies curriculum. Leaving the institute at the crack of dawn, we set off for the Sierra Nevada towards a place called Pueblito, the long-lost settlement of a once thriving indigenous civilisation. The bus stopped in a damp clearing by the Buritaca river, from where the mountain looked immeasurably high with its mist-covered peaks. Before our ascent, we were marshalled like soldiers by Arsenio Ruiz, our humanities lecturer and one of a handful of human beings with reliable knowledge of how to get safely to the legendary lost city of the Tayrona. Officially, the Sierra Nevada was the tallest maritime mountain range anywhere in the world, whose antediluvian tectonic roots were buried half a mile deep in the bottom of the Caribbean coast like colossal fingers. Above this a sophisticated ecosystem thrived with a seemingly endless variety of species in a diverse climatic habitat that included snow and perpetual ice caps at the summit. I looked up and remembered Georgiana describing her countless travel adventures with irrepressible enthusiasm. Having been among the first wave of foreign tourists to have explored the mountain, the intrepid English traveller had spoken to us of a lost city quite unlike any other she had encountered in either Mexico or Peru, the forgotten remains of an ancient civilisation concealed in the mountain by acres of rain forest and verdant foliage.

With barely contained anticipation, I set off to retrace her steps on a three-hour journey through an expansive area thick with vegetation nicknamed 'the green inferno', following a winding, ever-ascending mountain trail too narrow to accommodate the width of a donkey. I gradually noticed the temperature dropping and the air getting progressively denser and more rarified as we rose nearer to the top. Halfway along, we were granted a respite in a canopied shaded area, demarcated by a colossal circular boulder, where we could sit and catch our breath, stung by nettles and feeling like our legs and feet had been injected with liquid lead. The egg-like millennial stone, half-concealed by foliage and much taller than an adult, had been carved with glyphs apparently denoting the position of heavenly bodies, showing the Tayrona civilisation were no strangers to the functioning of the cosmos.

We continued our ascent through forests of green, occasionally distracted by flocks of toucans and colourful macaws flying in orderly formation against an immensity of emerald mountains, to the gentle murmur of cascading silvery waters. Finally leaving the jungle behind, we appeared to have entered a completely new world when we came to an orderly network of paved roads meticulously constructed with stone slabs. This led to a level area on the mountainside where a town had stood for millennia, featuring expertly built containing walls and hydraulic stone terraces that in ancient times had facilitated the irrigation of crops and supplied its population with drinking water, a powerful testament to the ingenuity of man in harmonious balance with the natural world.

"Guys, sit all around, make yourselves comfortable. It's time to hear what little we know about the people who built this place."

Arsenio Ruiz, a bright, animated man in his late twenties, was the most unlikely-looking teacher in our school. He would often turn up for lessons in trademark shorts and sandals and, with his long hair and beads around his neck, he was the epitome of what was commonly referred to as a hippie, complete with a long ginger beard and a *mochila* from which he would occasionally extract coca leaves to munch during punishing long mountain journeys.

"Eyewitness accounts of Spanish colonisers recorded an ancient civilisation that inhabited this land, a sophisticated civilisation in tune with the inner workings of this mountain. Then, for five hundred years, the location of the city remained a secret, until a lone mountain explorer accidentally stumbled on an urn containing treasure beyond the wildest dreams of modern man ... a funerary urn containing a solid gold mask and pectoral which he quickly sold on the black market... Unfortunately, this discovery kick-started an unprecedented gold rush. It didn't take long for thousands of *guaqueros*, a word used to describe treasure hunters and grave robbers, to make a beeline for this mountain in search of gold, a gold fever so ravenous and relentless that the mountain was soon stripped of all vestiges of pottery, beaded quartz jewellery and exquisite items made from jade and solid gold, many of which found their way into private collections and archaeological museums all around the world. As for the city's inhabitants... they disappeared without a trace a very long time ago. To this day, nobody knows the reason why or where they went."

I realised I was no stranger to the concept of people going missing unexpectedly and had in fact familiarised myself with the term 'the disappeared' from snatches of spoken exchanges between mother and virtually everybody who had opened their doors and taken us under their wing as we changed addresses with urgent frequency. So, it was with a mixture of irony and unease that I reflected on the ultimate fate of the Tayrona population. Whether they were forcibly uprooted and sent into exile nobody can be quite sure. All we know is that an entire indigenous culture mysteriously vanished from their millennial habitat and I, for one, found it ironic that certain individuals who disappear without warning from our lives are the ones who most tend to leave in their absence a haunting and long-lasting imprint. As for Georgiana, the intrepid explorer who had blazed a trail in our hearts like an errant comet, I still wished her all the happiness in the world despite her breaking her promise she would write to us from her green and pleasant land. Maybe mother was right and all things did have a cycle. Maybe the Tayrona had found a way to transcend life in their ancestral environment and finally moved on, leaving their wisdom and legacy behind for future generations to enjoy and, hopefully, learn valuable lessons from. This was how the journey to Pueblito – or Chairama, to give it its proper name – became one of my most abiding memories during a period in our lives when I still believed we would finally be blessed by lasting respite and calm.

Late November, 1979

Everybody remembers where they were when they first heard the news of the killing of Ricardo Gonzaga, investigative reporter for Radio Galeón.

"Let us get a slice of urban reality for a change", offered an unsuspecting Roger as he manoeuvred to change the cassette in the car stereo whilst driving me to the institute. Uncharacteristically for him, he had momentarily tuned into Aurelio Carbonell Estrada's early morning slot, something he was immediately to regret.

"This sad morning …" Carbonell intoned sombrely over the speakers, "we condemn the brutal killing of our erstwhile colleague and friend, Ricardo Gonzaga, an intrepid and fearless reporter who will be forever in our hearts …"

Roger immediately turned off the radio and the colour drained from his face. Forcing a smile, he turned to me and pressed play on the stereo, clearly intent on banishing the gloom. Music then blasted from the speakers.

"Nothing like some merengue early in the morning to lift one's spirits, eh buddy?"

In addition to being a well-known investigative reporter, Gonzaga had been a fierce opponent of municipal corruption. Having made something of a name for himself by lifting the lid on some of the most sordid aspects of Santa Marta's underworld, he was also deemed to have ruffled his fair share of feathers with his exposure of corruption within the higher echelons of local government. The previous night, Gonzaga had fallen prey to an unidentified gunman who approached him from a crowd, shooting him twice in the chest at point-blank range while the reporter was covering a public demonstration in a notorious quadrant known as Cuatro Bocas. Nobody was ever apprehended or claimed responsibility for his killing.

It may have seemed like a small detail, but what transpired in the taxi made a lasting impression. As Roger defiantly bobbed his head to the sound of the beat, a hint of anxiety on his face served as confirmation that the chiaroscuro world we inhabited was nothing more than a steady punctuation of rude awakenings from happy dreams we wished could last forever. From day to day we opened our eyes to a stark reality of contrasts consisting of light and darkness, rhythm and silence, joy and pain, exhilaration and anguish, right and wrong. Like the light of a brand new day, I slowly came to the realisation we were inconsequential little people endeavouring to make the right choices in a world where unseen and powerful forces of order and chaos were forever locked in a constant battle for supremacy.

CHAPTER 21

The Mirage

Early February 1980

The day came when I found myself training alongside my classmates on the school football pitch as part of our physical education class. The pitch itself was little more than an arid, dusty rectangular terrain encased by four high concrete walls at the back of the institute. It seemed to be a day like any other, except for an unusual headache which I blamed on the sun and the sensation of my heartbeat thumping in my ears, having sprinted behind the ball in an effort to prevent the opposing side from scoring. Right at the start of the match, I had also felt a sudden pull in my left thigh, a discomfort that continued even after requesting I be allowed to leave the pitch for a moment. 'Jaricho', our football coach and the father of Colombia's future World Cup team captain Carlos Valderrama, had himself been a professional player as well as a veteran of Magdalena's departmental football team and was therefore no stranger to sports injuries. He watched me for a few seconds before approaching me to address me in private: "If you aren't feeling well, lad, I think you'd better drink plenty of water and then go home. You look a bit dehydrated. Make sure you put some ice on that leg."

Having quenched my thirst from a tap on the wall, I picked up my backpack and, without changing from my sports gear into my clean clothes, began the long march back home under a inclement and temperamental sun.

Leaving the institute behind along the pedestrian route parallel to the same road Roger would use to drive me back home every day after class, I forged ahead covering the full length of the old market grounds, a flattened expanse of territory designated for urban development but provisionally being used as a municipal bus parking lot that bordered the new public market, and the old Escuela Normal de Señoritas, a colonial-style girls school run by nuns where mother had been a student in her teens, but which now looked abandoned and tumbledown, flanked by a series of dying palm trees. It was an area of inhospitable, desolate land where countless local businesses dumped their waste and where a population of vultures fed on dog carcasses scattered over the ground in various stages of decomposition.

I limped along a narrow road that led all the way home. Passing vehicles were strangely absent that afternoon and not a soul peered through any of the windows in the neighbourhood. The pain in my thigh increased as a searing heat filtered from the asphalt through the soles of my trainers. My addled senses were deceived by a constantly retreating mirage hovering above the incandescent road.

Shortly after arriving home, I succumbed to a deep sleep. Mother was alarmed to find me lying on the couch in the dark when she returned from work. After I had produced a brief explanation to mum about why I had come home earlier than usual, she placed a hot water bottle on my thigh, alternating it with a bag of ice cubes from the freezer. As the evening wore on, the pain in my leg got progressively worse despite strong painkillers. In a delirium, I heard Roger's concerned tone of voice during a conversation with mum outside of the house. He sounded extremely alarmed at not being able to locate me at the appointed time and place, having driven to school to pick me up. Making an effort to be discreet but failing to conceal the gravity in his tone of voice, Roger spoke of certain acquaintances of his who appeared to have gone missing without a trace. With that thought, I drifted off into an uncomfortable sleep.

Very early in the morning, mum put a thermometer in my mouth and detected a high fever. She immediately called the emergency centre and, before too long, we sped in the back of an ambulance to San Juan de Dios, a fortress-like hospital located in the southernmost part of El Camellón, by the sea and within earshot of crashing waves. I was dazzled by the sunlight as I was mobilised on a stretcher through the main entrance amid the deafening sound of loud voices in the area of accidents and emergencies. As soon as the doctors had determined that a massive staph infection had taken hold in my muscle tissue, they decided to operate immediately in order to save my leg. Applying general anaesthesia, they made me count to ten. I briefly awoke in the middle of surgery but next opened my eyes as I was being wheeled back from the operating theatre to a bed in a single room on the second floor where I was to stay for the duration of my convalescence. When later, full of curiosity, I removed the dressing covering my leg, I found an unstitched incision in my left thigh from where a long drain extended to a bucket collecting liquid. Before long, I was overcome by an uncontrollable seizure, the result of an adverse reaction to the general anaesthetic. Mum, who had been by my side all the time, held me tightly in her arms until the seizure subsided.

A few days later, on a sunny Thursday just before noon, Santa Rita Avenue was once again living up to being one of the busiest main roads in Santa Marta, where all manner of vehicles and public transport conveyances passed at various speeds along its two wide lanes. The Baboo clothing store on 22nd Street occupied premises on the ground floor of a low-rise building known as Edificio Los Andes.

The store itself was a small, air-conditioned commercial space, its walls lined with stained wooden boards, featuring an arrangement of exhibition cabinets stocked with folded denim and corduroy trousers for both men and women. A sizeable ornamental fish tank containing a variety of tropical fish adorned the back of the premises, leading to dressing rooms along a small back corridor. Beyond the corridor, the two employees had access to a small kitchen and a small warehouse space with boxes of merchandise, including a manual control to operate the air conditioning system and the sliding metal security doors.

It had been an arduous week that had seen mother juggling visiting me in hospital as often as she could and trying to adopt a more hands-on approach in the commission of her duties as the manager of the tiny clothing store. From within the cash desk enclosure in the middle of the shop by the window display of the latest summer collection, she had spent the first few minutes of her morning shift on the phone seeking to get an update from the doctor to check on my condition, since no direct calls could be transferred to any hospital patients. During a break following that morning's training session, she had unwound sufficiently to feel she could engage in animated chat with her two members of staff, fashion lover Ernilda Delgado, and football fanatic Eduardo Perdomo. The group of three stood gathered by the large window which offered a panoramic view of the uninterrupted passage of moving vehicles outside.

It had proved to be an exceptionally quiet morning for business and so the small group had allowed themselves a moment of relaxed banter while keeping an ear on the live football match being broadcast on the wireless. Unión Magdalena and Junior of Barranquilla, two of Colombia's staunchest football rivals, were playing a deciding match while the voice of the legendary Edgar Perea, an irrepressible sports commentator from Barranquilla, extolled the superiority of Junior over 'el Ciclón Bananero' in his inimitable broadcasting style through the shop's sound system that would otherwise be playing a mixture of salsa and disco music.

While the humorous cadence of Edgar's voice overpowered the debate between Ernilda and Eduardo as to the merits of both teams, which in turn provoked resounding laughter in the shop, mum's eyes suddenly focused on the moving traffic on the other side of the shop window. Amidst the seemingly endless procession of cars, buses and motorcycles moving along the stretch of Santa Rita avenue, she noticed a certain dark vehicle that appeared to have travelled along the same route on more than one occasion in a relatively short space of time.

Her eyes locked onto the car, which was now moving past the front of the shop more slowly than before. She briefly wondered whether a faulty traffic light was the cause of the slow pace on the road before realising there was no bottleneck in front of the car to impede its progress along the avenue. That was the moment she witnessed the smoked glass from the vehicle's right window being lowered.

The first thing she distinguished as the car window lowered was the silhouette of two men sitting in the front. The next thing she saw was the glint of the sun reflected on the barrel of a gun protruding out of the window and pointing in her direction. In a snapshot of past time, she somehow conjured up crystal-clear memories of the most pleasant moments of her childhood, as well as dreams and goals unfulfilled in her adulthood, while a cruel reminiscence of the long chain of events that had led her to where she now found herself reminded her of just how vulnerable and completely exposed she was. She was weary of living her life as a fugitive. The desperate manoeuvres and sacrifices she had made in order to ensure my protection during months of precarious decision-making traversed her subconscious in a tormenting parade of self-recrimination, her mood oscillating between the serenity of those willing to accept their fate and the absolute terror felt by those who want to survive.

The impact of the first bullet fragmented the glass in a spidery pattern before embedding itself into one of the cabinets at the back of the store. A sharp and desperate scream escaped mum's throat as she urged her colleagues to throw themselves on the floor. Before the three had reached the ground, a thunderous noise reverberated within the confines of the small retail unit as several projectiles of a different calibre completely shattered the display window, filling the interior of the shop with fragments of glass, pieces of wood and shreds of textile material. The deafening barrage lasted for less than five seconds, obliterating most of what was above ground level, including the cashier enclosure, the cash register, the telephone, the water cooler and the sound system.

Seconds later, all was quiet. A powdery debris lingered in the air, making breathing difficult. The fish tank and its contents had been scattered all over the carpet but the small group of three still lying face down on the floor refused to move. Absolute silence reigned for what seemed like an eternity.

CHAPTER 22

The President

It was almost impossible to conceive of the speed of the events that immediately followed the attempt on my mother's life. In the blink of an eye, the enduring sense of normality and stability that had anchored our lives up to that point had proven to be nothing more than a deceitful mirage that had plunged us into a false and dangerous sense of security.

In a matter of minutes, the Departamento Administrativo de Seguridad had closed off Avenida Santa Rita and diverted all traffic away from the crime scene. An ambulance was parked on the pavement at the entrance of the windowless premises where personnel from the ballistics department were busy gathering evidence, although it had not been necessary for the emergency services to transport anybody to hospital. Instead, the three traumatised witnesses who had suffered no more than minor cuts and bruises were ushered into an unmarked white van before being rushed to the DAS Agency located in an area of the city called Bavaria, in the hope they could assist the authorities with their inquiries.

The first thing Carmen requested upon arrival at the Agency was the use of a telephone to contact her lawyer, who promptly arrived by taxi in the company of Joaquina Serrano, childhood friend of my mother and the wife of Antonio Serrano Gómez, the Minister of Justice. As soon as the couple had joined Carmen in a room within the complex, she pleaded with her lawyer that absolutely no representatives from the media were to be informed regarding my whereabouts.

Oblivious to events outside my room, I continued convalescing in San Juan de Dios hospital and it remained uncertain whether the doctors would see fit to discharge me any time soon. Having completed her statement before DAS officials, Carmen then requested the presence of a notary at the Agency so she could give her lawyer power to handle on her behalf the deeds to her properties including the farm and the taxis still in her possession. She breathed a sigh of relief once all documentation had been rubber-stamped. Feeling more determined than ever, she looked at a petrified Joaquina and at Marco, who was already anticipating her intentions: "I need to call a press conference as soon as possible."

"For that to happen you would have to leave town first." Marco replied. "Now that your cover has been blown, neither the DAS agency nor any sane individual would recommend you stick your neck out again and make any more public statements. It's time you faced up to the fact you've run out of towns in which to hide. You are no longer one step ahead of them. And they've just shown you they're willing to resort to gangland methods in order to get you. The risk to your personal safety has become far too great."

Carmen looked defiantly at Marco, knowing he had a valid point. Clicking his fingers in the air in the manner he always did when fumbling for ideas, the lawyer spoke again: "I suggest you get an audience with the Regional Prosecutor to start formal proceedings against the State for acts of criminality."

Joaquina raised her eyebrows at the prospect of what was being invoked but Marco continued his reasoning.

"I know it's unprecedented, but the State Police have just tried to kill you. Napoleon and his men had probably been watching you for days. Nobody would begrudge you bringing the matter to the Prosecutor's attention… certainly not after what just happened. It's a miracle you and your colleagues were able to walk away from that mess in one piece …"

Carmen looked at the small cuts on her hands from the broken glass and at the front of her jeans that had barely dried from being soaked in water from the shop's shattered fish tank.

"What's more exciting, though …" Marco veered away from the subject, "I've been combing through all the paperwork I got from you in Bastidas and the case against the State is strong. I'm sure the Prosecutor will be glad to grant you a audience."

"That will mean me making an emergency trip to Bogotá", Carmen interjected.

Marco nodded with a smile. "Exactly."

Soon afterwards, an agent from the DAS intelligence service named Cristina was entrusted with Carmen's protective custody. The possibility of a covert journey to the hospital for mother to pay me a visit before her trip to Bogotá was briefly considered while an itinerary for her was being concocted in a bleakly illuminated office at the Agency in Bavaria. However, it was feared neither local authorities nor the discretion of hospital staff could be relied upon to keep my whereabouts a secret while I remained under medical observation. In view of the unfavourable logistics, both the lawyer and the DAS representatives organising mother's trip to the capital reached the conclusion that a quick journey for her to say goodbye to me at San Juan de Dios hospital was out of the question.

Overcome by a feeling of impotence and feeling she had no alternative but to accept being escorted out of the city at once for her own safety, Carmen asked to be left alone in the office. When the door closed, she began scribbling a long note on a sheet of photocopy paper she found on a desk. This very note would later find its way into my hands the day Marco Vinicio showed up in my hospital room accompanied by Joaquina Serrano.

Meanwhile, it was decided she would be leaving for the capital that very night, escorted to the airport by two DAS vehicles. Cristina showed up with a coat for Carmen to wear in the capital, and some personal effects. Bleary-eyed and with a haunted look that never again left her countenance, Carmen cast her eyes through the car window towards the cherished backstreets of her youth, reliving days when, as a carefree, barefoot teenager, she would join local boys for a football kick about after school before whiling away the night on a hammock to the sound of accordion rhythms under mango trees swaying in the tropical breeze. The shock of recent developments had not yet fully sunk in.

It was already dusk when a panoramic view of the long strip of the coast on the way to Simon Bolívar airport became visible through the car window. Soon the women were hurrying across the tarmac lit by the last golden rays of the sun before making their way up the passenger ladder to the plane, to the deafening whistle of its engines.

Before boarding the vessel, Carmen turned her head and just stood there in the breeze, watching the glow of the sunset reflected on the Caribbean Sea for one last time before being called to take her seat. Then, an air hostess slammed the door shut.

It was seven in the morning the next day and the act of opening my eyes when waking up was a slow and tortuous process. The nurse had left three different varieties of cereal and a jug of milk on the trolley next to my hospital bed. However, I was so drowsy, thirsty and dehydrated, that I gulped down the entire contents of the jug, which in no way lessened the repellent aftertaste of antibiotics. The impulse to go to the bathroom was so strong that I completely forgot that the drain dripping liquid into a tray by my bed was still attached to my leg, and my clumsy reflexes were too addled to prevent the container from falling to the floor with a loud racket.

Refreshed after a long shower, I decided to take my first walk outside the room and get to know the hospital by myself. San Juan de Dios was a large eighteenth-century yellow edifice that had first functioned as a convent and then as a hospital, the traditional birthplace of generations of *samarios*. Trying not to raise suspicion among the staff and holding the drain with one hand while trying to ignore the sharp pain in my thigh, I walked slowly along the corridor on the second floor from whose balustrade one could see a large atrium containing a lush colonnaded garden decorated with old cannons salvaged from the nearby coast.

During my solo tour, I discovered an empty room with a tiled floor, chequered black and white like a chessboard. Design and patterns, particularly those I found in architecture, had a reassuring, calming effect on me. The same was also true of board games, which, more than a hobby or a means of distraction, had often proved a therapeutic relief from frequent episodes of restlessness ever since Francesca had introduced me to the world of chess in the protective enclave of my old school's library. Keeping a tight grip on the tip of the drain with my fingers, I placed my feet on the tiles and slowly moved across each one of the square shapes. First, I imitated the movement of short-range pieces, beginning with those of the Knight and, finally, emulating the longer range of the Castle and the Bishop which, after the Queen, were the pieces with greater freedom of movement on the board. Just as I had started exploring the hypothetical escape options available to an embattled Queen, I heard the firm voice of a nurse who had been looking for me to replace the gauze on my thigh. Taking me by the hand, she addressed me in a strident tone as she led me back to my room: "Don't you disappear like that again. This hospital is far too big for someone as small as you."

The building, with its series of wide corridors, high ceilings, garden area did indeed dwarf everything it contained, including us. Some of the rooms resembled gigantic game boards that lent themselves to the enactment and illusion of a game of pure escapism.

My mother's arrival into Bogotá took place without incident. She and Cristina had not talked during the flight. As they were about to exit El Dorado airport, a handful of journalists stationed outside approached them as they hurried towards the car park. For the first time, Cristina spoke up, standing between mum and the group, saying firmly: "Please, gentlemen, make way for us, we really can't stop".

Without breaking their stride, both women got ready to board a DAS vehicle waiting for them outside with its engine running. Carmen acknowledged the correspondents who had gathered around the car.

"I have just this to say to the parents among you: if you have children, then please take good care of them."

As the vehicle negotiated the night traffic in the eternal drizzle of the capital, Cristina asked the driver if he could spot any of the correspondents on their tail.

Carmen said: "If they're following us, so much the better. That's what I came for. To testify openly to the press."

It took Cristina a few seconds to speak again as she kept an eye on the rear-view mirror.

"I second what you said about children back there… It's precisely the reason why I decided not to have any. To be a mother is to suffer constantly."

The DAS agent entrusted with her safety and the responsibility of getting them both to their temporary accommodation, was a woman in her early thirties, of strong build and pale complexion, with an oval face, green eyes and with the taciturn demeanour of someone reluctant to give their trust too easily. Carmen noticed that she was carrying a revolver under her jacket. The presence of reporters at the airport was also an indication that radio bulletins announcing the events of the last 24 hours had travelled quickly and the national press now appeared to be on high alert.

Their destination was a small hotel in a narrow street three blocks from Plaza Bolívar. Cristina checked them in at the small reception and the concierge carried their small pieces of luggage up a narrow set of stairs to a small high-ceilinged room on the second floor where somebody had somehow managed to fit a double bed. From the limited vantage point afforded by a window covered with wooden blinds, Carmen was just about able to survey the activity of passers-by and traffic below while Cristina disappeared into the adjoining room. Carmen had only just begun processing a plethora of emotions that had accumulated over the course of a seemingly endless day. Although she was still wearing a thick wool sweater under the waterproof trench coat Cristina had given her and her breath was easily visible in an alien coldness making her tremble with anxiety, she resolved to maintain her composure between the anonymous four walls that now surrounded her. Once again she approached the window and saw the dimly illuminated street below. The buildings across the street barely afforded her the sight of more than a tiny piece of grey night sky. At that moment, she felt lonelier than ever.

She never knew when she eventually fell asleep but she was rudely woken up by the noise of the morning traffic and the first thing she did when she jumped out of her bed was to rush to the window expecting to see the press reporters that had followed her to her current accommodation which from time to time had been known to house individuals under the witness protection scheme. Her intuition proved correct, as she immediately spotted a handful of men with cameras around their necks standing in front of the premises. One of the reporters was distributing coffee in polystyrene cups to others stationed in the cold of the morning. She then glimpsed Cristina on the pavement approaching the hotel carrying a shopping bag. Without stopping, she stared at the correspondents before entering the hotel. A minute later, she knocked on Carmen's door and gave her a can of soda, salt crackers and some pieces of cheese for breakfast.

"There's a swarm of journalists across the street," she said seriously as she produced a thermos flask full of smoking black coffee.

"Good", Carmen replied, "I was keeping an eye on them. In a few minutes I'll go down and talk to them."

Meanwhile, that same morning, Marco Vinicio showed up in my hospital room with Joaquina Serrano, the wife of Antonio Serrano Gómez, who at that time was serving as Minister of Justice. I was finding it hard to keep my eyes open and, upon realising I could not speak coherently due the effect of my prescribed medications, the couple decided to hear what my doctor had to say.

"The infection caused some inevitable loss of muscle tissue in his leg" he said, but we expect him to make a full recovery."

The noise of trolley wheels carrying surgical utensils heralded the arrival of the nurse who had come to apply a fresh gauze to my leg. I winced as I felt her icy hands on my thigh and opened my eyes for the first time, taking a long look at the incision which resembled a yawning mouth.

"How did you spend the night, champ?" Marco exclaimed keenly.

I immediately asked about my mum, whom I hadn't seen since the day she had held me tightly in her arms during the seizures triggered by the general anaesthetic. Noticing my discomfort, Joaquina, an elegant brunette lady with well-kept bouffant hair and smartly dressed in black, smiled sweetly at me. Leaning forward and taking me by the hand, she spoke in a voice that resembled a lullaby: "Your mom had to leave the city for a while … for work reasons …"

For a moment, I suspected Joaquina was trying to distract me from what the nurse was doing until I saw her take a sealed envelope out of her handbag.

"Before she left, she told me to give you this letter. She realised she couldn't call you so she wrote you instead. She hasn't stopped thinking about you."

Exchanging a look with Marco, she concluded: "And we won't stop coming to visit you either. We will be here for anything you need."

Not to be outdone, Marco added "The stuffed *arepas* they sell in the old quarter will make your mouth water. I guarantee you'll never want to touch hospital food ever again!"

As soon as all the adults had left the room, I ripped open the envelope and began to read:

Dearest son. This will be the last time you and I are going to be apart. Do not fear, for I have left good people to take care of you in my absence and provide you with anything you might need. Remember that conversation we had the other night? Well, once again I must beg you to be patient for a little while longer and, most importantly, to remain strong. Even if, yet again, my occupation demands that you and I are separated for a short space of time, just like the cycle of water, things will soon return to the way they used to be. I assure you all the sacrifice of these last couple of years will have been for the best.

Meanwhile, nearly a thousand kilometres away to the south, a press conference with representatives from all the main newspapers was in progress.

"First of all, can you explain to us who these 'birds of prey' are that radio bulletins from your part of the country keep referring to?"

Carmen was seated in a corner of the foyer next to the hotel reception, surrounded by half a dozen journalists either standing or in their respective chairs. In the photos that were eventually published of her in the press, mum featured dressed in the same beige trench coat she had worn since her arrival at El Dorado airport. She also wore a head scarf that covered her hair in its entirety and dark glasses to protect her eyes from the flashes of the photographic equipment. The question had come from a correspondent for the newspaper *El Bogotano*.

"It's a denomination, a nickname made popular by the tabloid media to refer to a group of vigilantes responsible for the execution and disappearance of a large number of people over the years. This is no urban legend. Bodies of petty criminals mostly from disadvantaged communes increasingly continue to be found all over town. Many turn a blind eye to this, some may even rejoice in the social cleansing aspect of it, which is abhorrent in itself. But the fact remains no one dares to address the issue in the open for fear of reprisals. As a civil servant, I was able to gather sufficient evidence to prove that the group responsible for these extra-judicial murders are in fact active members of the F-2. Having been threatened by my superior, I took to the airwaves to publicly denounce their kidnappings and homicides. My radio interview was quickly followed by my summary dismissal and sparked incessant efforts by F-2 agents to find my whereabouts all over town in order to silence me. Had it not been for the courage of selfless members of the community continuously offering me their protection in various ways and risking their own physical integrity in the process, I would not be here in your midst talking to you today. Having narrowly escaped an armed attempt against my life in broad daylight scarcely 24 hours ago, I have every reason to believe that these individuals will stop at nothing until they have killed me."

"That's quite a serious accusation to level at our state police. Have you thought about applying for political asylum abroad?", asked a correspondent from *El Tiempo*.

"Not at all. I have no intention of leaving this country. I still feel I have a job to do and an obligation as a mother to fulfil right here. And if this accusation against our state police appears in any way inappropriate to any of you, then let those in the highest positions of command condemn or take responsibility for the sudden disappearances of Georgiana Ellis-Carrington, Diego Alberto Jesús Andrade and a gentleman everybody knew as Forero, just three of the victims I had come to know on a personal level, whose bodies have never been found to this day. Meanwhile, the list of the dead and the disappeared just keeps getting longer and longer. Have you thought about how frightening it is to raise children in a society where law enforcement entities are nothing more than a cover for rapists and murderers?"

Half an hour later, the two women were back in Carmen's hotel room, sitting on the edge of the bed, immersed in their own thoughts while they finished off the contents of a tin of water biscuits washed down with the remaining black coffee from the thermos flask.

Cristina was the first to break the silence: "If I get wind that anything like that is going on at my agency, I will seriously be reconsidering my position."

For a second, it occurred to Carmen to inquire whether the DAS operative had any motive to suspect levels of corruption within her own agency. Instead, she resigned herself to offering advice she hoped would prove timely: "Whether you think anything may be happening or not, by all means follow your instincts, then make sure of your facts. You have given up many rights as a woman to be in a position that allows you to make a real difference in this world. Do not simply walk away. We need more people like you."

The following day, after a sleepless night spent staring at the black crossbars in the ceiling of her room, the telephone on the bedside table began to ring. She jumped up in a split second but was glued to the edge of her bed, unsure whether to take the call. Apart from Cristina and the coordinators of the intelligence service who had made arrangements for her stay at the hostel, she was certain no one else knew her exact location within the building, much less the telephone number of her room. Despite her apprehension, she lifted the handset.

"It's Antonio. I'm calling from Washington DC", announced the familiar voice on the other side of the line: "Don't be alarmed. It's one of the safest telephone lines, we can talk about anything. I am in DC as delegate for an anti-narcotics event and have just heard the news of your press conference via Radio Cuba. You are taking a tremendous risk. However, I congratulate you. I wouldn't have expected any less from you."

Antonio Serrano Gómez was acting Minister of Justice in Colombia, having earlier come to prominence as Defence Attorney in the Supreme Court of Justice in the higher courts of Bogotá. Carmen's friendship with the jurist and his wife Joaquina extended back to the days of his election campaigns when he sought to be elected as Chief Senator for the Magdalena region, a position he held three times in a row.

"Listen, I just had a word with my wife. She visited your son in hospital along with your solicitor. She wants you to know the boy is doing great and is in good spirits, he is recovering quite well. Also, Joaquina tells me you're seeking a hearing with the Prosecutor to start proceedings against the State. In my opinion, he will take forever and judicial processes are ridiculously slow. But there might be another way. I will see what I can do. I'll talk to you again tomorrow."

During the two days that followed, Antonio's morning calls were a much welcome boost to her morale after an endless succession of dead ends that imbued her with a sense of isolation and loneliness.

"I'll be flying to Bogotá tomorrow. And since you are in the capital, I'm sure you'll be pleased to learn there's a space available in the protocols agenda at Casa Nariño this week. If all goes well, it's very likely I can arrange for you to have a face-to-face meeting with the President."

20 February, 1980

The last telephone communication from the Minister of Justice, which appeared to come from a walkie-talkie, was the briefest of announcements, a message so succinct it could have been tailored as a telegram:

"You have an appointment at Casa de Nariño for eleven in the morning later today. I will come to collect you in a few minutes."

Carmen hung up the phone and realised she had to relay the news to her police escort and prepare for the trip to the Presidential Palace six blocks away from the hostel.

She sat in the waiting area where just a few days ago she had fielded questions from reporters from a variety of national newspapers. Even without the presence of people, the room felt an oppressive and claustrophobic space.

In a matter of minutes, the jurist and minister arrived in a chauffeur-driven official car. Antonio Serrano Gómez was a charismatic Creole with short wavy hair, whose ease of expression and warm cordiality instantly earned him the trust of everyone who came into contact with him. His dark suit, polka-dot tie, polished shoes and dazzling smile seemed to dispel the morning gloom.

"How are they treating you here?" he asked, as he greeted Carmen with a hug under the watchful eye of Cristina, who observed proceedings from a corner of the reception area while the vehicle's engine hummed outside. "I think we can give your escort a break while you and I see that you get to your appointment. I can't wait to catch up with you properly."

They crossed the narrow cobbled street in front of the hostel and got in the back of the car together, with its strong smell of new leather inside.

"The truth is your declarations to the national press took everybody in the cabinet by surprise, including the President himself. As far as I'm aware, he has something in mind for you at the palace. Something positive. Although I'm not entirely sure exactly what it might be." Antonio digressed and briefly reminisced on his role in the cabinet with renewed enthusiasm. "We have decided to put an end to the mafia's involvement in our politics once and for all. We've spent the past two years redefining this country's security policies from the ground up. It means going back to basics from a legal and constitutional point of view, that's how young we still are as a nation. Not all of us see eye to eye when it comes to reforms, it's true, but as usual we do so with the very best of intentions."

For a moment, Carmen wondered what he meant by security policies needing to be 'redefined from the ground up'. Before she asked him to elaborate, the conversation came to a halt when the vehicle slowed down and the imposing neoclassical façade of La Casa de Nariño became visible. They continued slowly along Seventh Avenue until coming to a stop in front of the white gates of the building's old entrance, where a uniformed guard was stationed.

Antonio Serrano was the first to leave the car, closely followed by Carmen. The Minister of Justice tilted his head towards the guard who, acknowledging the signal, opened the gate to admit the two visitors. Having entered the main building, they followed another uniformed guard along a hall adorned with a twin set of large oriental vases on both sides and illuminated by baccarat crystal lamps. Passing an old statue of Italian marble flanked by two columns, they continued up the main stairs and came to a momentary stop in front of a spacious room furnished with upholstered yellow French armchairs, where visiting diplomats presented their credentials.

Antonio turned to Carmen and said: "They will inform the President you are here."

I woke up again for what seemed to be the fifth time that morning, wanting to change position but still restricted by the drain attached to my thigh. The nurse entered the room with a fresh supply of sterile gauze and proceeded with the daily routine of redressing my wound. In seconds, the smell of alcohol saturated the enclosure.

"How are you, champ?" I heard the voice of lawyer Marco Vinicio Suárez as he walked into the room wearing his usual square-rimmed glasses and a short-sleeved guayabera shirt. But the first thing I noticed was the brown paper bag full of hot corn *arepas* cupped in his hand. Smiling from ear to ear, he placed the bag on the bedside table and the seductive smell of corn reached my nostrils. His agile mind immediately noticed my attention turn to the bundle of newspapers he carried tucked under his arm, and in an effort to distract me, he quickly referred to one of my favourite hobbies: "I also brought you crossword puzzles to entertain you. This will stop you from talking to the nurses. We don't want them getting so distracted they leave a pair of scissors inside your leg."

With dexterity and speed, he reached for the bundle, pulled out the crosswords pages from their staples, and placed them on the chair beside me.

"Eat your *arepas* while they are still hot." He looked on intently as I munched away, reminiscing on the occasion I had had my tonsils removed in the same hospital when I was five and was forced to eat flavoured jelly for weeks afterwards. He leant towards me and whispered conspiratorially as he tapped me on the knee. "You will come out of this one and many more".

The two of them continued along a corridor where the walls were being papered over by uniformed contractors and where a strong smell of varnish addled the senses. As Antonio observed the activity of workers carrying decorating materials and carefully transporting pieces of historical value such as framed canvases and ancient vases, he turned to Carmen and laughed: "It's taking longer for our administration to redecorate the interior of Casa de Nariño than to put the finishing touches to our country's own constitution!"

Antonio intimated further: "The President is a well-intentioned man with a firm commitment to restore stability to our nation. In your case, I am confident he will do the right thing by you."

Arriving at a hall reserved for protocol events, with walls decorated with finely woven tapestry, the two sat on large French armchairs and waited to be called by the President, under the scrutiny of a closed circuit television camera.

Shortly, a well-dressed woman with a clipboard appeared at the entrance to the room. Calling Carmen by name, she politely requested she accompany her. Adjusting her trench coat as she began to feel the cold inside the building, Carmen turned her gaze towards Antonio in the forlorn hope her friend would accompany her to her audience with the President. Instead, he looked at her from where he was sitting and, perhaps in an unguarded effort to impart encouragement, uttered a phrase that very aptly denoted the magnitude of the task that now lay before her: "It's your struggle. It has always been your struggle."

After following the woman down the corridor and through an impressive rectangular doorway, Carmen was ushered into a large room. The door closed behind her with a click. A polished wooden floor reflected the light of a large crystal chandelier hanging in the middle of the ceiling and at the far end of the room, next to a large Colombian flag fastened to a pole, was an enormous wooden desk flanked by two chairs upholstered in polished red leather.

To the right of the room, by a window adorned with red curtains, stood a large man dressed in a grey suit, whose serene countenance transmitted a calming beatific stare through a pair of square-rimmed glasses. Turning towards Carmen, the twelfth President of the Republic of Colombia extended his hand in a gesture of greeting.

"Welcome to Casa de Nariño. It is an honour to have you here with us. I want you to know we are extremely grateful for the valuable service you have rendered to our nation."

His slow, rather colloquial manner of speaking was little more than a whisper. "Please excuse the appearance of our house. We are still in the process of renovating. It will all be finished soon, though."

Resting on a marble coffee table was a silver tray with half a dozen china cups arranged around a steaming teapot.

"I brought a selection of teas to help fend off the low temperature inside this building. Let me know your preference and I will bring it to you. In the meantime, please take a seat in front of the desk."

Placing a cup in front of her, he carefully poured hot water through a strainer containing tea leaves, the steam infusing the air with a fragrance of jasmine. Carmen thanked him for his kindness. For his part, he continued smiling and, holding the ends of his bow tie between index finger and thumb, said: "We are always at your service."

Finally taking his seat on the other side of the desk, the President began rummaging through some documents he had taken out of a drawer on his right.

"Let's see what we have here. Oh, yes … Nurse, Municipal Comptroller's Office, Córdova Infantry Battalion No. 5, National Police. An impeccable resumé. Which is why we have decided to make you the following proposal.

You have certainly proved to be a civil official of rare integrity in the fulfilment of your duties. I have no doubt you are the ideal person for the position we have in mind."

As he spoke, the President continued turning the pages like someone playing a delicate stringed instrument.

"There is currently a vacancy in one of our embassies abroad. We thought that maybe we would have to wait a little longer to grant that privilege to someone equally competent, but at this moment in time I can't think of anyone more suitable for that position than you."

Joining the palms of his hands, he resumed speaking in the same slow whisper.

"Let's get to the heart of the matter. I am offering you a diplomatic position at the Colombian Embassy in Madrid. We will need your cooperation abroad for the next four years. Obviously, it is my duty to inform you that this diplomatic role will cover little more than my current presidential term. However, we hope you will make yourself available for the position with immediate effect. The necessary arrangements for your departure as well as protocols to ensure a harmonious transition to your new post should all come into effect by the end of the week. Of course, we would only need your written consent here in the presence of my officials, but it is a straightforward formality we can finalise immediately."

Meanwhile, I had been administered yet more antibiotics and it looked like I would be left alone again in my room for a while. I took mum's note out of the envelope and read it for the umpteenth time. There was that word again: 'sacrifice'. Of all the words in her note, it was the one that struck a dissonant chord with the overall sentiments of reassurance. As far as I was aware, the sale of her cars, the lease of our family house and everything pointed to her being in financial difficulties. Was she having to work in a different city in order to make ends meet? Once again, I decided to leave my room for a walk in an effort to clear my mind, this time with the drain in my thigh safely secured under a newly applied gauze.

Outside, a group of nuns came by, like giant pepper pots gliding silently along the wide corridors of the hospital. I attempted to walk as inconspicuously as possible while trying to ignore the aftertaste of penicillin in my palate, the chess manoeuvre of the 'Queen's Sacrifice' firmly embedded in my mind. I quietly wondered whether, as adults, it was our lot in life to make stark choices, to be constantly forced to explore every available avenue in order to find solutions to problems while confronting our worst fears along the way, not unlike pieces in a game driven by players endlessly devising strategies to reach their destination while keeping out of harm's way. I therefore wondered what defences were available to a Queen coming face to face with her most crucial challenges.

"Mr. President, with all due respect, allow me to express my surprise and immediate concern regarding your proposal. I sit before you as a former officer of the National Police. And I stress 'former', not in the sense of someone who has wilfully or willingly given up her privilege to serve the nation, but as someone who in the commission of her duties suffered endless persecution at the hands of her former colleagues, all active members of the F-2, for daring to denounce unprecedented levels of corruption and criminality within the service carried out with continued impunity and on the watch of several administrations of the Colombian government. Let me remind you that, in the eyes of justice, no one is above the law, that, as law-abiding citizens of a civilised society, we are all equally deserving of compassion, dignity and respect. Which is why I continue to insist that all irregularities that led to my uncovering all manner of heinous acts of police brutality, which resulted in relentless persecution against me be properly investigated and condemned, the perpetrators brought to justice and, lastly, that I be reinstated in my role as a civil servant so that I may continue to serve the country that I love."

For a few seconds, the President watched Carmen in silence with the same beatific smile he had shown from the beginning. She observed the movement of his hands through the steam rising above the intact cup of tea, as if he was shuffling an invisible deck of cards.

Driven by a sense of unfinished business, I found my way back to the room with the black-and-white tiled floor that made me think of a giant game of chess, the same place where I had sought to distract myself by playing a game on my own before being unexpectedly interrupted by the nurse. As I had used to hear Francesca say at my old school – no doubt seeking to prepare me for adulthood when I already knew adulthood was overrated – the game of chess very much resembled how grown-ups lived their lives. Not unlike a game of soldiers, even if I preferred my soldiers made out of paper and stuffed with sweet treats. If it resembled adult life, then it was a brutal game, for adult life was a game where participants could be trampled under the hooves of injustice, while others ended up being confined within the walls of tall towers as punishment. A game where bishops made grandiose pronouncements loaded with fire and brimstone and where pawns made sure there were always obstacles along the way. It was also a game where participants were made to disappear. A game where, in order to win, it was not uncommon for embattled Queens to make sacrifices, even though, as I had always believed, there surely had to be another way.

However, my blood froze when I found the huge wooden door to my secret game room had been locked. Out of frustration, and with the portals of my primary school education in my mind, I compulsively traced a rectangular figure around the door. For a brief moment, I felt transported back to Bogotá, the night I searched for an exit from my own confinement. A way out from a world that had ceased to make any sense and, if not exactly a world ruled by villains at the expense of the good guys, certainly one propelled by a capricious and uncaring providence.

Ruled by a sudden sense of unease, I walked down the stone stairs all the way to the ground floor, in pursuit of reassuring geometric figures. I had found many a solution to bouts of anxiety was achieved through the calming effect of games. Games such as checkers, or Snakes and Ladders – preferably with toboggans instead of snakes. Ignoring the frantic activity of paramedics and hospital personnel coming and going around me, I scrutinised the floor in search of familiar patterns, only to find disorder in all the disparate designs I encountered, their randomness foreign to my understanding and as far removed from the more familiar black-and-white patterns now denied to me in a locked room two floors above. I realised the futility of following established rules in pursuit of a game whose current state of play had become a mystery. Instead of recognisable structures, what lay before my eyes was chaos and disorder, a mess of asymmetrical designs in complete disarray, the equivalent of someone changing the goalposts overnight. In vain I endeavoured to find a vestige of logic in the amorphous Byzantine patterns where established rules had been subverted to the point that they now held no validity or meaning.

"I'm afraid that's not quite how our state mechanisms work," the President finally replied. "To begin with, it is our country's law that determines how corrective measures, or any other function similar to those, are to be effected. We mustn't overstep the line or deviate from those established parameters. That is the way of madness. Our intelligence service is as indispensable for our country as the air that we breathe. It would be foolish and downright dangerous to demand that our established instruments of security suddenly be restricted or overhauled in any way. Not for a second. Our very freedoms are dependent on the continuous functioning of our intelligence service at all times of the day and night."

"Mr. President, of course the intelligence service is there to safeguard our freedoms and our institutions, after all that is its primary function. But it becomes a threat when its *raison d'être* becomes distorted, when it is led by corrupt people who, if left to their own devices, transform it into a mechanism of insecurity and fear. The least that your administration could do is to keep a watchful eye on those in command of the intelligence service and then act accordingly. You talk to me about our law, but I have it on good authority that, as a country, we still don't have any properly delineated statutes for our security and defence. As it stands, the first guidelines of a Statute of Security have barely been drafted by your administration and, therefore, there is no way to interpret a law that does not yet exist. What is abundantly clear, however, and as someone who for years has stood on the frontline and witnessed all manner of atrocities being perpetrated by those supposed to be upholding the law in our streets, is that a purge of our existing intelligence service has become necessary as a matter of urgency. It is extremely vital that our very own instruments of security are not subverted and abused by those who believe themselves to be untouchable and with carte blanche to commit all manner of criminal acts and gross extrajudicial violence with impunity."

"That is true, but only to a certain extent," the President deadpanned in the same slow tone of voice, but with an authoritarian cadence that had previously been absent until then. "It is true that we have very delicate social problems in our hands. Which is why we remain grateful to people like you for helping us identify some of those ... rotten apples. However, it is important to remember that anomalies of that kind are in a minority. Of course we are not saying we have finally been able to weed out every single vestige of corruption from our institutions. What we can say is that we have an ongoing policy, a will to act, and that we are more than willing to face those difficulties and take the fight to those very few still giving our institutions a bad name. But it's an ongoing process and we are certain to succeed if we keep our nerve."

"Mr. President, my loyalty to justice has been my top priority throughout my life. I have an impeccable service record. Rest assured I will never cease to be faithful to the oath I took right from the beginning as an official of my government. So far I have managed to honour that oath against all odds and in spite of the clear and present danger to my physical integrity. Since my youth, my goal has always been and will continue to be to serve my country in the best possible way, to the best of my abilities and in accordance with my own conscience.

However, I am also a single mother, with a minor who needs my attention and constant support ... a child I am still trying to bring up to embrace values we hold dear so that one day in a not too distant future, when he is a fully formed adult, he may become an exemplary citizen. This requires I continue to be present for him until he is able to fend for himself.

Therefore, I sit before you today, beseeching you that I may be allowed to resume my duties as before, in the service of my country, without my basic rights as a citizen continuing to be trampled by murderers holding positions of power in our own National Police.

As for the diplomatic position you offered me ... it would be wholly inappropriate for me to accept it. The reality is I have no diplomatic competence of any kind. That much you know, as you hold my resumé in your hands. Therefore, I am afraid I am unable to accept your offer of a diplomatic position abroad. Let us not forget, however, the long catalogue of injustices continuing to be perpetrated here in our own country by our own authorities, all of which constitutes nothing less than a national disgrace.

From now on, whatever you decide will be of utmost importance for the health and stability of our nation. Until now, we have been witnessing an endless cycle of social cleansing and the systematic destruction of lives in my region, some with potential repercussions abroad. Any decision you make today will inevitably have ramifications for our country. We have endured too much suffering for long enough. Now, it is up to you to finally do what is right ... And your conscience will be clear, not because you will have chosen the easiest or more convenient path forward. Your conscience will be clear ... simply because you will have done what is right."

The President's air of benevolence had now vanished. He turned his eyes towards the large freestanding clock on his right as if wanting to know the time and, for a moment, seemed confronted by his own reflection on the polished lacquered surface of his enormous desk. Suddenly, he stood up from his presidential seat, inattentive and in the manner of someone whose mind was already set on other matters.

"Thank you for coming", he uttered matter of factly before walking from behind his desk and, without pausing, crossed the length of the room and headed towards the door which he held open. He then addressed Carmen for one last time.

"It has been a pleasure."

Rising from the red leather chair, Carmen made her way slowly across the shining wooden floor and walked through the door that the President was still holding open for her. As she exited the box-like threshold that separated the presidential office from the corridor outside, two uniformed contractors approached in her direction, carrying a massive rolled carpet between them.

"Ah, gentlemen ... Enter carefully ..." she heard the President say as she walked away down the hallway.

"And, please, make sure the space where the floor reflects the light of the chandelier is completely covered by the carpet ..."

Short of breath and with her temples palpitating to the accelerated beating of her heart, Carmen navigated the length of the corridor with the heaviness of someone wading through treacle, invaded by a cold that froze her to the marrow. When she met Antonio in the waiting room, no exchange of words was necessary for him to realise she was blown apart, her despondency transparent in her sorrowful countenance.

Sitting down in the chair she had occupied earlier, she exhaled resignedly: "They want me alive. But only as long as I'm abroad and too far away to cause any further nuisance. Now I know they would much rather have seen me dead, here in my own country."

Antonio watched her with concern, uncharacteristically silent and unsure what to say.

"You're in no condition to leave here on your own", he finally ventured. Walking towards a window, he produced a portable transmitter-receiver from his jacket pocket and called his driver who was stationed on Avenida Séptima.

"Gerardo", he said with urgency, as he kept an eye on the close-circuit camera in a corner of the ceiling, "we have a situation".

Carmen's eyes were fixed on an exquisitely ornate porcelain vase positioned on a table, unusually adorned with a stuffed, forlorn-looking beetle that had left numerous tracks around the lacquered base, stubbornly determined to continue its tortuous march in a spiral of infinity.

She did not know how she found the strength to walk down the staircase watched over by an enormous portrait of El Libertador Simon Bolívar, who appeared to keep track of their progress from the top with a penetrating, watchful gaze. Flanked by white columns, five flags stood in a line along the ground floor: one representing the country's Air Force, another one the Army, followed by the flag of the Navy, that of the National Police, and lastly, in the centre of them all, the flag of the General Command, integrating all the Armed Forces of the country. Carmen thought about her years of service in the Infantry Battalion and the premature end of her career as a member of the National Police. For a moment, she stared at the symbols of the nation with wistful eyes, as if suddenly oblivious as to what they truly represented.

Leaving the row of flags behind, she took out her scarf from her trench coat and tied it around her head. Outside, they were greeted by a gust of icy wind while portentous groups of grey clouds moved rapidly across the sky of the capital, blocking every nuance of light and creating moments of near darkness. Stopping for a few seconds, she turned to Antonio, as if carefully choosing her words.

"I know your hands are tied. And I know that you cannot persuade the President to do anything differently. He had clearly made up his mind in advance about what he wanted from me and appears to be firmly entrenched in whatever ideas he has for the future of the nation. However, if anything were to happen to me, I implore you to take care of my son."

Antonio looked at her with surprise, struck by the uncomfortable irony of being the Minister of Justice and yet, skilled as he was in the power games of politics, a law-maker whose responsibilities included the prevention of potential attacks on state security assets by subversive groups, he now felt powerless to guarantee the physical security of one of his own citizens, much less ensure the safety of a minor. Even so, he was sufficiently emboldened by the unshakeable friendship he shared with Carmen for him to feel he was more than up to the task: "Whatever happens, rest assured that I will look after your boy."

Strong glacial winds fiercely buffeted the high plateau of the Andes as the two of them went through a small courtyard decorated with pots of geraniums before they left the palace complex through a security gate, into the street, right where Antonio's car was waiting for them with its engine running.

Antonio's skilful jurist's mind carried on exploring all the possibilities available to them.

"We'll look for a diplomatic route. I know someone who may prove useful to us. Ricardo Galán is the current Ambassador of Mexico. I can take advantage of his presence in Bogotá, as he's due to arrive here in a couple of days. We could start exit procedures for you right away to get you to Mexico. As drastic as it may sound, the idea of seeking asylum in another country is not all that crazy. You need to be somewhere safe to rethink your life. And it's quite clear it's no longer safe for you to stay in Colombia."

He looked at Carmen with a palpable air of regret: "I'm ever so sorry."

Wind-assisted hail bursts pelted the surfaces of the vehicle, hampering visibility as it drove away. Lowering his guard for a moment, the Minister of Justice betrayed a growing unease with his role in the current administration: "I hope I'm wrong but now that the country has taken this course, I fear we may soon be staring into the abyss."

A few hours later, in the city of Santa Marta, preparations were underway for Director General of the Police Manuel Méndez Mantilla to hold an emergency press conference:

"Let me be clear once and for all. The F-2 strongly rejects this woman's version of events ... The reckless allegations this person has been disseminating through many media outlets are completely false. This city welcomes lots of tourists on a daily basis, including some from abroad. And you know what? None have ever gone missing! It is interesting to note that this person claiming to be a former F-2 official does not even appear in any official records of any departmental or state entity ... So let our communities carry on as usual. Let our citizens pay no notice to ... rambling accusations intended to tarnish the good name and reputation of our police institutions. They have clearly been concocted by a delusional mind. That's all I have to say. Thank you very much."

That same evening I was awakened from a short but deep sleep by the sound of waves coming and going, crashing repeatedly against the rocks on a nearby pier. For the first time since my admission to hospital, I felt stable enough to climb one of the chairs in order to reach the tiny square window high up the wall of my room facing the sea. From my precarious perspective to the outside world I felt the breeze on my face and contemplated the breathtaking spectacle of a sunset over the Caribbean Sea, a kaleidoscope of bloody colours constantly varying in intensity.

At the same time, nearly a thousand kilometres to the south, Carmen silently watched the night fall from the sky from the confinement of the concrete cage of her hostel accommodation, struggling to distinguish a tiny portion of metallic grey sky from the vantage point of her solitude.

CHAPTER 23

Exile

Late February, 1980

Throughout his life, Albert Stanton was noted for his unerring punctuality. Today, however, he sat motionless and perplexed in front of the steering wheel of his car in the middle of a road in Bogotá, shaking his head from side to side in disbelief at the static line of vehicles through his windscreen. It was Wednesday 27th February, and there were only a few more minutes to go before the start of a reception for diplomats at the Embassy of the Dominican Republic to which he had been invited.

Mr Stanton was Head of Chancery and Principal Coordinator of the British Embassy in Bogotá and also acted as General Officer for the Diplomatic Service Overseas Inspectorate. He would subsequently be appointed Director of the Nuclear Energy Department in the Foreign and Commonwealth Office.

That fateful afternoon, however, he felt like one more obstacle in the middle of another notorious traffic jam in central Bogotá. Not being someone to stand on ceremony, he smiled at how ridiculous he felt in the impeccably tailored tuxedo he had persuaded himself to wear for the occasion. He glanced at his watch for one last time and, knowing he had been thoroughly defeated by the Bogotá traffic, looked around for the quickest way out. As soon as he detected a slight forward movement of the vehicle in front of him, he rapidly turned the steering wheel of his car and manoeuvred his way out of the line of vehicles, going over a central reservation as he effected a U-turn. He then drove in the opposite direction back to his hotel, leaving the insurmountable metropolitan thrombosis behind.

In retrospect, the traffic setback proved to be a fortuitous outcome for Stanton. Just five minutes after his decision to abandon the tailback to return to his hotel, a certain group of individuals who until then had been seen playing an innocent-looking game of football on a strip of grass across from

150

the city's university campus stormed the Embassy of the Dominican Republic the moment the United States ambassador had begun welcoming diplomatic guests. Rapidly mobilising from the grass strip a few metres away, the attackers, who carried concealed firearms under their clothing, broke into the residence where some fifty people had gathered, firing shots at the ceiling and taking hostage for the next sixty days almost all the diplomatic personnel who were in Colombia. Thus began 'Operation Freedom or Democracy', masterminded by the subversive group M-19, the most serious diplomatic incident the country had witnessed.

Having parked his car in the hotel car park, Stanton headed to his room to change into something more comfortable. An envelope containing a telegram from the Ambassador of Mexico rested on his bedside table. Without opening the envelope, he put it in his jacket pocket before taking the lift to the bar, thinking of ordering a Scotch and feeling quite relieved at not having to rub shoulders with the other diplomats at the Dominican Embassy. Entering the hotel bar, he encountered the peculiar spectacle of groups of people standing perplexed and mostly silent, their eyes glued to a large television screen transmitting an assortment of black-and-white images and live footage as the siege was taking place inside the embassy.

As for Carmen, her visit to Casa Nariño seven days before had been followed by a succession of sleepless nights, and every waking hour spent in the confinement of her hostel accommodation increased her lethargy and anxiety. Privy to this and making a conscious effort not to disturb her, Cristina now limited herself to leaving a tray of daily provisions outside her door.

28 February, 1980

That Wednesday morning, Carmen woke from a deep sleep when she heard the sound of footsteps outside her room. As she turned her head, she spotted something small underneath the door. Dragging herself out of bed, she approached the door and bent down to pick it up. It appeared to be a business card bearing an unfamiliar name: Albert Stanton, British Embassy.

She turned it over and read a brief handwritten message in blue ink: "Please take a look outside your window."

She spotted a large black car parked across the street from the hostel with two small flags on each side. One of them was the flag of the United Kingdom.

She put on her coat and, almost stumbling upon Cristina as she left her room, the two women walked together down the narrow stairs and went out into the street.

"I didn't want to wake you", Cristina said by way of explanation. "Besides, the ambassador said he was willing to wait for you outside to avoid disturbing you."

One of the side windows in the rear of the vehicle lowered until the silhouette of a person was visible. Noticing Carmen's apprehension, Cristina turned to her: "It's okay. I verified he's from the British Embassy. He handed me the card I pushed under your door. I'll be watching you from here."

A uniformed chauffeur emerged from the vehicle and opened a rear door for Carmen as she crossed the narrow street. Sitting inside the back of the car was a middle-aged man with Caucasian features, of affable manner, who spoke in fluent Spanish.

"Good afternoon, madam. Allow me to introduce myself. My name is Albert Stanton, Head of the Diplomatic Service." He wore a pair of spectacles and a Scottish tweed jacket that gave him the air of a university professor.

"I apologise for giving you such short notice but what brings me here is a matter of the utmost importance. If you don't mind, I would like to talk to you in private."

Glancing over her shoulder at Cristina across the road, Carmen adjusted her trench coat before decidedly entering the back of the vehicle. The driver then closed the door after her, eliminating the noise of street traffic.

"This morning I received a telegram from the Mexican ambassador informing me that you possess vital information regarding the whereabouts of Georgiana Ellis-Carrington, a British citizen who has been missing in Colombia for nearly three years. Unfortunately, I only read his communication following the takeover of the Embassy…"

For a few seconds, Carmen sat staring at him in astonishment.

"Oh, I see…", realised Stanton, for the first time betraying an English accent in his pronunciation. "Your companion tells me you have not left your room for a week. I suppose you continue to be oblivious to the situation."

Carmen looked in the direction of a cafeteria a few yards away from the hostel where she saw Cristina buying provisions and having her thermos flask filled with fresh coffee. She then turned to the diplomat.

152

"Mr. Stanton, Cristina is my guardian from the intelligence service. While you wait to hear what I have to say, perhaps you can assist me with meeting the Mexican Ambassador? The Minister of Justice assured me he would be arranging an audience with him for the purpose of processing my departure to Mexico, since my life is in jeopardy in this country".

Carmen had barely finished her sentence when she heard a tapping sound on the car window.

"The donuts from the intelligence service have arrived", announced Cristina, carrying a bag of groceries. "Get them while the getting is hot".

Cristina's skills as an agent included an almost uncanny ability to read lips through tinted car windows and to approach parked vehicles unnoticed. Opening the passenger door, she sat herself down in the front passenger seat and turned to Carmen with a summary of the day's news: "The M-19 took over the Dominican Embassy this morning. They're holding about sixty hostages inside the building, including the Mexican Ambassador."

For a few moments there was a deathly silence inside the vehicle, until Cristina began handing out cups of steaming black coffee to the passengers.

"It's an extremely delicate situation," the diplomat added. "Several close colleagues of mine are among the hostages."

Following another pause, during which those in the car sipped their coffee while Carmen simply heated her hands with her cup, the diplomat spoke again: "I will be brief. And I apologise for turning up in an official vehicle, but I am obliged to use it for embassy matters. Regarding the disappearance of the British citizen, I'm afraid the government of your country has proved less than helpful and what little crumbs of information we have managed to extricate from the local police has led us to a dead end. For my part, I would be extremely grateful if you could help us gather some facts."

Carmen did not hesitate to answer: "Of course I'll help you. That's precisely why I am here in Bogotá, to talk about the many who have gone missing or have vanished without a trace."

"In that case", said Stanton, "I would be delighted if you would accompany me to the British Embassy. We are ready to take an official statement from you."

After a lengthy journey that took them north of the capital, the driver finally parked the official vehicle by a grey, box-like multi-storey building. The three passengers took an elevator that emerged directly into an austere, sparsely decorated room with large windows. Here they were met by two suited individuals sitting on a sofa behind a coffee table.

"These gentlemen are here to gather your testimony", Stanton said, introducing them to each other. "Please take a seat here. I will act as interpreter. We know the girl originally came to this country via the Andes on a tourist trail that finally took her to Santa Marta before her disappearance. Since then, the Colombian authorities have consistently denied any knowledge of her whereabouts."

One of the men switched on a tape recorder and the diplomat asked Carmen to begin her statement.

"Mr. Stanton. Gentlemen…" Carmen began, as she looked into the eyes of each of the individuals sitting in front of her, aware of the magnitude of what she was about to say.

"Georgiana Ellis-Carrington is dead. She was kidnapped and murdered by state police operatives in the city of Santa Marta nearly three years ago."

The British officials did not need an interpreter to understand her words. They looked at one other as if they were at last getting confirmation of what they already knew to be true. Standing by the door, Cristina looked through a window at the grey panorama of dark clouds above the capital, as Carmen recounted the fateful day the unfortunate girl showed up at the F-2 headquarters asking for help and the chain of events that led to her murder. She described how two of her former colleagues had bragged about the atrocity and she revisited the petrifying confrontation with her superior and subsequent dismissal from the force, her years of service removed from public records followed by more than two years in hiding with her son from relentless persecution by the police. Carmen poured out her heart irrepressibly, each sentence a maelstrom of condemnation of the rapid debasement of her country's institutions and labyrinthine levels of corruption reaching the highest echelons of power.

Carmen's last night in the hostel felt like a repeat of all the others: lying sleeplessly in her bed, overcome by mental fatigue. She was staring at the prison-like beams of the ceiling with a sense of déjà vu when Cristina urged her to pack her few belongings, as apparently the time had come for her to be relocated to other accommodation. First, however, Stanton wanted to see her one last time.

Without looking back, the women got into a DAS security white van and set off on a twenty-minute journey to meet with the British diplomat, who cut a lone figure standing by the entrance to the hotel which, like most parts of the capital, seemed uncharacteristically deserted, since most of the population were glued to their television screens. He approached to greet them as they stepped out of the car. "Good morning to you both."

In response, Carmen only managed to say: "Mr. Stanton…"

"Please call me Albert," the Briton replied warmly. "And once again thank you for agreeing to meet me at the last minute." He then turned to Cristina and asked her to come back for Carmen in forty-five minutes.

Leaving behind the white security van, they walked through the lobby to the hotel bar. Around them was the tense spectacle of groups of people captivated by the ongoing events of the second day of the siege of the Dominican Republic Embassy unfolding live on the large television screen behind the bar.

"I've taken the liberty of reserving a table for us, away from the bustle of the bar. What I have to tell you is for your ears only."

From their table at one end of the restaurant it was still possible to glimpse at an angle the huge television screen transmitting live images of the periphery of the embassy. A waiter presented them with a breakfast menu. The Englishman ordered a ginger infusion while Carmen asked for a cup of black coffee to warm her cold hands.

The diplomat epitomised the idea some may have of an English gentleman, complete with pin-striped tie and glasses below his ample forehead that made one think of a retired academic. As he stirred the contents of his cup with a teaspoon, he spoke again in near perfect Spanish with just the slightest vestige of an accent from his native Tunbridge Wells.

"I have been in communication with the British intelligence service," he said in a soft voice, as if describing a casual occurrence. Placing a teaspoon on the side of the cup, he continued: "Based on what we were able to establish thanks to your statement, I have been granted full authority to lead an operation to apprehend the suspects of Ms Ellis-Carrington's murder."

While the diplomat was speaking to Carmen, six hundred miles north of the country, a convoy of six vehicles silently advanced along the Caribbean coast from the city of Barranquilla. Stanton took a look at his watch.

"At this precise moment, the arrests of each one of the suspects are being carried out by members of our intelligence service with the participation of DAS."

After parking their vehicles on 13th Street of Santa Marta, members of the SIS and the DAS entered the headquarters of the F-2, taking Lieutenant

Carrasco by surprise and dragging him out of his office in handcuffs before astonished members of staff. Seven other suspects were also similarly rounded up and apprehended.

"As you can imagine" Stanton said sympathetically, "the young woman's parents have waited years to hear news of her daughter. Perhaps now they will finally be able to put an end to this tragic episode."

In that instant, Carmen was convinced she heard a crystalline laugh reverberating from a distant past, and the memory of a smiling, carefree young woman dancing in her eastern regalia, her long hair shimmering in the light of the living room. She also recalled the occasion Georgiana stood on tiptoe with a radiant expression of glee to place the glittering paper star on the top of their Christmas tree, causing both mother and son to burst into applause. Taking the cup to his lips, the diplomat added with a melancholy air:

"At least her parents will no longer have to endure further uncertainty and will be extremely grateful for any additional information you may be able to provide regarding their daughter. In order for that to happen, you would first have to give your consent to be transferred to the United Kingdom."

"Mr Albert … before you continue, may I remind you I have a son convalescing in hospital hundreds of miles away from here. I currently have no means of contacting him". For a moment, she cast a look at the groups of people standing in paralysed clusters around the room watching silently as the siege at the embassy continued to unfold, the light of the television screen flickering on their bewildered faces. "Forgive me but I am finding all this quite hard to process."

"Yes, of course you are understandably concerned. However, allow me to allay your fears once and for all. I have been made aware of the situation with your child through your friend, the Minister of Justice. Due to the ongoing situation at the Embassy, Mr Serrano Gómez rightly observed that Mexico was no longer an asylum option for you, as originally intended. However, I am pleased to inform you that, as from today, arrangements are underway to ensure your son is fully protected and supervised until he can be reunited with you in England. I have been given specific assurances by your friend that this will be the case."

"Our country will continue to offer you assistance and protection as may be necessary, in addition to granting you full British citizenship without prejudice – a chance for you and your son to start anew and rebuild from all this. Of course, you must consider this not as an imposition but as a formal request from Her Majesty's government."

Stanton stretched out his hand. Undecided, Carmen took a few moments to block out the constant stream of live bulletins amidst the growing tension inside the room. She thought about her son for a few moments before finally acquiescing in a gesture of agreement.

"On behalf of my government", Stanton stressed, "I will make it my responsibility to oversee your unhindered transfer to the United Kingdom with immediate effect. The latter will be carried out as soon as the Ministry of Foreign Affairs has granted its permission."

At last Carmen gave free rein to her pent-up emotions.

"Thank you for restoring my confidence in justice!", she sobbed.

Then, recovering her composure sufficiently to accept the handkerchief the diplomat offered her, she said: "I've been living like an exile in my own country. A country I am sad to say I can no longer call my own."

29 February, 1980

Carmen's trip under escort to El Dorado airport and the unprecedented operation to extricate her from the country was carried out with the utmost speed and minimum of fuss. Tangible evidence of her departure is an archived transcript of a conversation between two British SIS agents who accompanied her on her journey across the Atlantic, acknowledging that their "charge" was "on her way". For many decades afterwards, she would still relive that flight across the Atlantic as one of the most heartbreaking and loneliest experiences of her life.

Meanwhile, hundreds of miles to the north of the country, the time had come for me to be finally discharged from hospital, that colonial edifice with its balustraded passageways and central Franciscan cloister that for weeks had felt more like a juvenile penitentiary than a recovery centre.

At noon that day, Antonio Serrano Gómez and his wife arrived in fulfilment of a promise he had made to mum that he would take care of me in her absence. He presented me with a cardboard box containing the largest pizza I had ever seen in my life.

Once all the relevant paperwork was sorted out, the couple took me by each hand towards the tunnel-like exit of the institution, where I was greeted by a fresh sea breeze and bathed by the light of the afternoon sun for the first time in weeks. Antonio's personal driver – whose nickname was 'The

Roadrunner', after the *Looney Tunes* series of animated cartoons, on account of his ability to safely negotiate busy roads in the shortest space of time without crashing – patiently waited for us in an all-terrain air-conditioned van. During the journey, Antonio gave me my very first pair of sunglasses, which I wore throughout my trip to what would be my last home in Colombia.

Our destination was a two-level colonial-style house in a neighbourhood called Las Acacias, with pristine white walls covered in bougainvillea, a crescent-shaped driveway and a main entrance decorated by enormous terracotta pots. Despite the lingering discomfort in my leg, I got out with a sensation of new-found freedom, aiming to absorb my new surroundings with the curiosity of an explorer.

Regarding the outcome of the siege of the embassy of the Dominican Republic and the 52 days of negotiations that followed, the government agreed to grant the guerrillas of M-19 safe passage to the airport along with all the hostages to Cuba. Part of the agreed terms included the release of all kidnapped ambassadors once the plane had touched down in Havana. Although it was never corroborated by either side, the guerrillas obtained an indeterminate sum of money from the Colombian government. Subsequently, and through a specially drawn-up peace treaty, the M-19 became a political party whose leaders came to occupy high positions of state.

Following the release of the hostages on 30th April 1980, President of the Republic Julio Cesar Turbay Ayala proclaimed victory through the media and cemented his place in the annals of Colombian history by promulgating the slogan with which he sought to summarise the legacy of his '*paz bélica*' ('Bellicose Peace'): "We all won. The entire country won."

In less than a year, however, the dark clouds of organised smuggling and drug trafficking would cast a permanent shadow over the nation for the next four decades. The Statute of Security that the Turbay administration had tentatively drawn up in order to repress the actions of subversive groups, including those of the M-19 urban guerrilla, was modified to impose draconian rules of state on all citizens, at one stage contemplating the implementation of martial law, causing outbreaks of indignation in academic sectors and protests in international communities. A concatenation of systematic corruption and unwarranted compromise in the highest echelons of power had finally opened a Pandora's Box of uncontrollable dark forces.

The intensification of guerrilla activity and the advent of narco-trafficking that gave rise to the likes of Pablo Escobar and the notorious Orejuela Clan were about to turn the country into a more violent and more complex place than ever before.

The nightmare scenario forewarned by a lone desperate voice who had flown to her exile had suddenly come to pass.

CHAPTER 24

War Tribunal

Mid-March, 1980

"It's a fourteen-syllable word!" asserted Antonio Jr.

"No, it only has thirteen!" countered Antonieta, his sister.

"Oh yeah? Count the syllables as you repeat 'Supercalifragilisticexpialidocious'. Slowly. I think you'll find it's actually fourteen!"

Whenever their parents were out for the night, the Serrano siblings and I enjoyed marathon viewings of undubbed movies from the households's video library. As soon as one of those tapes disappeared into the anonymous silver box, we would huddle together on the beige pile carpet of the master bedroom, sticking our heads out from beneath the king-size bed like soldiers peering out from a bunker, watching in rapture the adventures of a flying nanny called Mary Poppins, singing along to *A Spoonful of Sugar* or *Feed the Birds*, while the brother and sister, who were already on their way to being bilingual, would take every opportunity to correct my pronunciation. As coincidence would have it, the last movie we saw together was Disney's production of *Peter Pan*, prominently featuring Big Ben, where the cartoon version of that landmark looked very much the way Georgiana had drawn it on a scrap of paper seemingly a century ago.

"'The second star to the right and straight on till morning!'" the siblings shouted in unison when Peter and the children stopped at the iconic clock face before flying to Neverland.

"You'll soon be making the same journey when the time comes for you to fly to London!", Antonieta enthused.

My stay at the Serranos was a temporary measure until travel arrangements could be finalised for me to rejoin my mother abroad. However, it had not taken long for me to be accepted as a member of the family. For living necessities and privacy, I was granted the use of the guest room at the top of house which had a partial view of a manicured patio with a small hut for

160

drinks and barbecues, as well as a private swimming pool. The young daughter of the Serranos proudly introduced me to her collection of Barbie dolls which came complete with a selection of disco and ballroom outfits. Her brother would let me borrow one of his spare bicycles after school and, just before supper, the three of us would be allowed to enjoy carefree outings within the confines of the neighbourhood along rows of coconut trees in the glow of the afternoon sun.

Together, we would stop just within the perimeter where the road leading to the edge of the southernmost part of town was perennially busy with traffic: family cars on their way to El Rodadero beach resort, yellow taxis, cargo lorries and busloads of tourists. At other times, we would survey parts of the neighbourhood, an exclusive urban housing complex built by the United Fruit Company during the days of the banana trade bonanza, which included a splendid Club House, tennis courts and its own private hospital, a home from home where American landowners of regional farms growing cocoa, tobacco and sugar cane would wander around in their smart white linen suits and Panama hats, having arrived by steamship from New Orleans. Clutching state-of-the-art cameras, they made silent mini-movies of local inhabitants going about their business, black-and-white footage that would later be projected onto outdoor screens in remote coffee plantations such as 'Cincinnati' in the Sierra Nevada, to entertain labourers and their families in their evening breaks.

Fast forward to the present day and, away from prying cameras of any description, a trial was about to take place within the confines of a military compound, an event that was to shake the nation's institutions of law and order to their very foundations.

Early June 1980

"The sunlight outside the shop was too bright…" reflected Sarmiento on the microphone. "It didn't matter how many times we drove around the block, I just couldn't get a proper shot from the car."

More than a hundred kilometres west of Santa Marta, the final hearing of the War Tribunal at the Ejército Nacional Intendencia Local de Brigada No. 2 against members of the F-2 was underway in the city of Barranquilla. On trial were eight individuals who disgraced humanity with their existence.

The trial was an event that laid bare the underbelly of institutionalised abuse of power in the country's law enforcement machinery, with shameful repercussions on a national and international scale.

Lieutenant Carrasco, ex-chief of police and one of the prime suspects, vigorously protested that the trial "undermined the nation's ability to eradicate crime at its source". Speaking into his microphone, prosecutor Horacio Salcedo countered: "Does your notion of 'eradicating crime at its source' include vigilante-style homicides on an unprecedented scale? If so, what shall we call the premeditated kidnapping, rape and killing of an innocent young tourist? Let us take a moment to discuss Miss Ellis-Carrington, who for months had been reported missing by the British Embassy – for the record, an anomaly that had been publicly denied by the Director General of the Police. Can you enlighten us as to how her remains ended up in a specific location in the outskirts of the city, a discovery only made possible as a result of a tip-off to the British Ambassador by a former officer of your unit while she was still on the run from your henchmen?"

The harsher the scrutiny of the nation's instruments of intelligence and security, the bigger the cracks on the crumbling edifice of the state which now groaned under the accumulated weight of its transgressions.

"In this diagram", indicated the prosecutor to those present in the chamber, "we can see the exact geographical location that the F-2 operatives gathered here today in this chamber had designated for the disposal of the girl's body. A remote site outside the city, more specifically the bottom of a well that, following an inspection by a team of forensics, subsequently yielded fragments of human bone as well as remains of teeth that were later found to be a precise match with Miss Ellis-Carrington's dental records in the United Kingdom."

Addressing Carrasco, whose face had by now been drained of all colour, the prosecutor continued. "Let us now talk about the fate you had prepared for Carmen Monzón, your former employee and the person who, having called a press conference in Bogotá, first brought to light the National Police's streak of kidnappings and extrajudicial executions in this part of the country. Instrumental to this process was the documentary evidence that this female ex-officer had managed to compile against you during her last weeks of active service, before you and your men had her marked for persecution and murder. Crucially, and following an examination of the scene of the assassination attempt on Ms Monzón, the ballistics report from DAS established that military-grade ammunition of a type used by the Armed Forces, including men in your unit, had been used in the drive-by shooting, thereby ruling out any involvement by the mafia or any subversive organisation. Unfortunately for you, this particular finding points directly to you and your accomplices as being the main perpetrators."

On the second day of the trial, an ex F-2 operative named Sarmiento was in the process of testifying against his own colleagues in exchange for a reduced sentence.

"Agent Vergara over here procured the houses … where the, erm, victims … were tortured at leisure prior to being executed."

"That's pretty rich coming from the torturer-in-chief himself", interjected Vergara from an adjoining table.

"Any further interruptions to proceedings and those responsible will be removed from the court room to solitary confinement", admonished the judge.

Sarmiento continued: "Agents Valverde, Vergara, Arango, Cristancho, Montoya and Pérez… would all take turns to abuse the girls that were taken into custody… Agent Valverde in particular, had an unhealthy obsession with female prisoners… Suspects young or old, mostly young miscreants, met grisly ends at the hands of these men. Locating suspects was my main assignment but, as a God-fearing man, I myself chose not to take an active part in any of these atrocities, let alone what Valverde and the others did to that innocent foreign female…"

While he was still talking, the Military Criminal Investigation Court N. 68 witnessed the spectacle of Valverde who, without any warning and having somehow broken away from security staff, clambered swiftly over the tables and wrapped his handcuffs around Sarmiento's neck, before being forced to the ground by bailiffs. Such was the savagery of his resistance that it took the combined strength of four army personnel to immobilise him. A decision was therefore made to continue the remainder of the trial by telephone line.

When the judicial process was finally brought to its conclusion, seven of the individuals were sentenced to a combined total of 280 years in prison, without any chance of parole. The aftermath of the trial was quickly followed by a nationwide wave of revulsion and condemnation of the F-2, while human rights observers from around the world kept a watchful eye on the country's response to the unprecedented ruling. A belated act of contrition on the part of an embarrassed government finally led to the permanent dismantling of the State Police's most notorious branch.

Justice had also caught up with Manuel Méndez Mantilla, Director General of the Police. Having spared no efforts in hindering all sincere attempts to bring transparency to the conduct of law enforcement across the country, he himself was found guilty by the Supreme Court of Justice and sentenced to a total of 30 years in prison for 'friendly links' with paramilitary leaders, as well as for his role in the assassination of Luis Carlos Galán, cartel-fighting candidate for the presidency of Colombia.

Back at home in the sedate environs of Barrio Las Acacias, a daily routine had developed whereby the Serrano kids and I would have breakfast together and either exchange riddles or practise English before being driven to our respective schools and then back later to the solace of the family household.

As for Mr. Serrano Gómez, I would catch precious few glimpses of him, engaged as he was in constantly shuttling between his government job in Bogotá and Santa Marta, and the few occasions I was to see him in the house were punctuated by me pestering him to allow me to have the daily crossword puzzle from *El Espectador* newspaper, a copy of which he always brought along with him from the plane.

One afternoon like any other, while I noticed the Justice Minister appearing more immersed in his thoughts than usual, as he sat in his brown-leather reclining chair in an impeccable beige suit while tinkling the ice cubes in his customary glass of Scotch whisky, he suddenly stood up and walked towards the tiny office next to his bedroom from where he produced a wad of newspapers he had been keeping in a draw of his mahogany desk imported from Florida.

"*Chico*, it's about time you were finally made aware of a few important matters."

Editions of national newspapers carefully concealed from my eyes for weeks now lay on display before me on the desk. A number of them featured images of my mother's face splashed prominently on their front pages, some under sensational headlines (in Spanish) such as 'Police Woman Sentenced to Die' and 'Former F-2 Operative may have Sought Asylum Abroad'. Unable to speak, I felt a sudden chill in my veins as if a veil was being lifted from my eyes, signalling the exact moment my childhood irrevocably slipped away.

I finally came to realise why mother had emphasised the need for me to remain strong. Contrary to what I had long suspected, her sacrifice had not been caused by a sudden reversal of fortune or unexpected economic setback. As we frantically shuttled from place to place seeking refuge, she had made every conceivable effort to keep me distracted from the harsher aspects of life. I was made to realise in an instant that no amount of therapeutic enactment of games could shield anybody forever from the cruel vicissitudes of this world.

I looked carefully at the clumsily retouched ID image of Georgiana's face that the sensationalist media appeared to have procured from a distorted facsimile and which some editor had decided to publish alongside a photo of my mother. I tried in vain to associate the strangely artificial facial features on the front page of the newspaper with the lively flesh-and-blood girl from overseas who had enlivened our household with her exuberant charm and *joie de vivre* during her fleeting time in our lives.

For days on end, the newspapers kept me company in the solitude of my room upstairs. On returning from school I would run up the banister stairs to lock myself in the world of that room and compulsively re-read what I had already read the day and night before. I would remain awake for many a sleepless night and watch the sunrise from my window, longing for the cold early mornings at the farm by the Sierra Nevada and the tranquillity afforded by the murmur of crystal clear waters cascading down the neighbouring ravine.

Back in the real world, the sordid reanimation of Georgiana Ellis-Carrington from her ashes by the tabloids in their daily ritual of sensational reportage catering to the lowest common denominator had been an unedifying spectacle that threatened to remove all vestige of her humanity. By the end, I had navigated through all the different stages of grief and the simmering sense of outrage that had accompanied me for days had finally given way to a feeling of numbness and emptiness.

Winds of change were announcing themselves across the Atlantic litoral region as they usually did around the end of every year. The first leaf storm of the season was gathering speed outside the house as I sat by the half-moon-shaped driveway expecting to see scores of Edwardian nannies being blown away beneath darkened Caribbean skies. It was the night before my flight into the unknown to the other side of the world and it occurred to me to approach "The Roadrunner", the household's private chauffeur, who could be spotted in the driveway struggling to light a cigarette during a break from work. I asked him if he could drive me to Mamatoco in the SUV he used for running errands, so that I could say goodbye to my grandmother. His jaw dropped as he processed my unexpected request but he soon realised I was serious.

"Let me run this by the boss first", he said as we both walked towards his employer's small office. Like everybody in the household, the driver was aware that my time in Colombia was coming to an end. As for me, the urge to visit my grandmother's house one last time had become as vital a necessity as breathing.

"You are to bring him back in less than thirty minutes", came the response from Antonio Serrano, who looked in my direction with a hint of camaraderie and the unspoken concern of someone weighing up the possibility that something might just happen to me on the eve of my flight.

Having been given the green light to leave the house under escort, I enthusiastically sat next to the driver, who turned on the engine before setting off from Las Acacias on a frantic journey that saw our vehicle buffeted by strong winds along Avenida del Libertador on its way to my timeless, beloved village just outside the city. It had been dark long before our departure and the annual meteorological phenomenon of trade winds approaching all the way from the Atlantic was making its presence felt with increasing ferocity. As we sped over Mamatoco bridge and swerved left by the entrance to San Pedro Alejandrino, a sudden power outage plunged the entire sector into an abyssal darkness.

By now nothing but the howling wind could be heard and, save for a faint glow flickering to life through one of the windows in grandma's old yellow house, no light of any other description could be seen anywhere in the vicinity when the SUV came to a standstill by the house. I ran as fast as I could and prised open the heavy wooden front door which grandma usually kept unlocked. I quickly ran to the lounge where grandma spent much of her downtime on her artesanal rocking chair and there she was, the picture of austere elegance in a patterned black-and-white dress, rosary in her hands and a single freshly lit candle at her side. I didn't stop until her face was next to mine:

"Grandma" I uttered, suddenly struggling for words "I came to say goodbye... I'm leaving the country first thing tomorrow and I'm not sure if I will ever return."

I leaned over her and tightly embraced that body of tremulous old flesh, gently running my fingers through her cotton-white hair and feeling the warm moisture of tears descending through deep furrows on her kind, ancient face which I would never see again.

Knowing time was running out for me before I was due back to Las Acacias, I ran from room to room along familiar straw mud corridors I could sort through with my eyes shut, even in the near-complete darkness, passing relics and porcelains without slowing down as I bid farewell to anybody in the house who could hear me.

Continuing with the same momentum, despite hearing the driver tooting his horn outside the house, I carried on running until I was in the middle of the yard, now glowing with an eerie nocturnal light, surrounded by the plants and fruit trees that had witnessed my frequent forays from everyday reality. I had returned to my favourite refuge of tranquillity, a place now being transformed and rearranged by increasingly strong winds that appeared intent on erasing any evidence of an idyllic past and where swarms of fireflies endowed the dream-like panorama with an otherworldly charm.

Finally, I climbed on top of the large, round, wooden lid of the well that supplied the house with drinking water, a place I would often enjoy jumping from despite my long-suffering grandma's protestations and, for the last time, I looked up and stared at the nocturnal immensity of that familiar Caribbean hemisphere whose configuration I knew like the palm of my hand. Driven by an irresistible impulse, I raised both my hands towards a starry black sky, wishing to cradle an immensity of constellations and fireflies stubbornly persisting in their celestial dance with their intermittent lights until the last one of them had been blown away by the wind.

CHAPTER 25

Neverland

January 1981

I was woken abruptly by the air stewardess tapping me on the shoulder insistently. Opening my eyes, I found an imposing woman in uniform talking to me unintelligibly. With a sigh, and finally realising I was unable to understand anything she was saying, she quickly fastened my seat belt before disappearing down the narrow aisle just as the plane began its descent. I turned to look through the window and could only make out groups of rapidly passing black clouds through a film of condensation.

The landing on the runway made the entire plane shake with a crunching thud. I had finally arrived in London, England.

The day before, I had spent my final hours in Colombia whiling away the time at the airport in the city of Cartagena de Indias until the time came for me to board my flight to Miami unaccompanied. Just a few hours earlier I had said my farewells to teachers and friends alike, the intimation being I was to be away for a short while. In my bones, however, I felt like a tree being uprooted, waiting to be replanted in an unknown remote corner of the world. To his credit, Marco Vinicio unexpectedly showed up unannounced on the doorstep of the house in Las Acacias, apologising profusely for not having checked on me earlier, having been prevented from doing so by a court case that kept him away in Barranquilla.

"Promise you will tell me more about that!", I asked.

"Yes, of course. I promise to write you and your mum in more detail. And I think I'd better stop now before my big mouth gets me into trouble", he chuckled.

"I will write you a postcard with Big Ben on it".

"Now that you mention writing, this is for you", he perked up, handing me a small box containing an expensive Paper Mate pen as a parting gift, adding with a smile and a wink: "Just my little way of ensuring you return the favour, champ".

Reminiscing on past events that were to conclude with my relocation to another continent, I realised I had barely given myself any time to process the bulk of what had happened. It was already midnight as the plane crossed the Caribbean towards Florida for a scheduled connection to a long journey across the Atlantic.

"The second star to the right and straight on till morning", I said to myself, as I looked at the night sky through the window, before succumbing to a dreamless sleep.

Following the announcement that we were finally being allowed to disembark, I felt the temperature plummeting with each step I took through the tunnel that connected the aircraft to the Heathrow airport terminal, a sensation exacerbated by monumental jet lag. Passengers walked past me as I stopped to put on more wool jumpers thoughtfully given to me by the Serranos in preparation for my trip. By the time I joined the queue for border control I was wearing as many layers as an onion. Nervously producing my travel documentation for the official to inspect, I could feel my good fortune dwindling when airport staff exchanged quizzical looks and decided to retain my passport.

I was then led away by the hand to an adjacent small room where I was interviewed in English by two immigration officials.

"He arrived unaccompanied on a Laker plane from Miami."

"Why did you come to the UK?"

"I've come to be reunited with my mum", I replied, with the help of the Spanish interpreter that had been brought in.

"What do you mean, you came to be reunited with your mum?"

Before I could give an answer, I began to hyperventilate from an asthma attack. As I fumbled for my inhaler in my hand luggage, an official in a suit unexpectedly entered the room: "It's alright, this little chap can come along with me. His mother and her solicitor have been in touch and they're waiting for him at Arrivals."

Full of expectation and with a renewed sense of hope, I advanced alongside the official through anonymous empty corridors. Reinvigorated and propelled by the now familiar sensation of butterflies in my belly, I quickened my pace like a marathon runner spotting the finishing line, along a cold, grey tunnel terminating in the morning glow of the waiting area marked Arrivals. And there she was, wearing a beige coat and beaming with irrepressible emotion.

I immediately ran in her direction and, as we put an end to an unbearable absence with a prolonged embrace, I felt I was home again. As once foretold by Georgiana, I had finally reached my final destination, a journey that had started four years ago in the patio of our former house as an innocent therapeutic board game, when the world was still full of endless possibilities. As mother wrapped a woolly scarf around my neck to protect me from the freezing air, I wondered whether home was really about inhabiting a specific location in the world, or whether it was in fact a sanctuary of the mind, a nurturing environment where certainty and trust dominate over chaos.

Standing next to mum was her solicitor, an amiable, venerable looking moustachioed gentleman in a heavy brown coat, who greeted me cordially in Spanish and who, having filled in all the necessary documentation on my behalf, was patiently waiting to guide us to the exit. Outside the airport, flurries of snow covered every available surface with a blanket of pristine white as we boarded a London black taxi. On our way to the big city the snowstorm intensified and the bright headlights from other moving vehicles could barely be seen coming and going along the motorway in the greyness of the day. As we warmed each other's hands in the back of the car, it occurred to me to ask mum how near her house was to Big Ben and whether families set time aside for flying kites together in the park. Somewhere in South London a new beginning awaited us.

EPILOGUE

September, 2015

One early autumn morning on the second weekend of September 2015, more than thirty-five years since our arrival in the United Kingdom, mother and I feel a sharp cold breeze on our faces as we sit side by side warding off the low temperatures on a public bench by St Thomas Tower, while contemplating the River Thames, that ancient, winding thread of silvery liquid splitting the city in half and following a serpentine course as old as time itself.

Clusters of people have been steadily gathering to witness the annual Thames Festival, looking attentively at the flotilla of colourfully decorated ships sailing around Tower Bridge, that marvel of Victorian engineering. However, I only have eyes for one particular ship.

I watch the elegant vessel as she sails through the open bascules of the bridge, a resplendent ship with tall masts, a shiny black hull and huge sails swollen by the morning wind. Far from being the forlorn, ghostly apparition most art lovers are familiar with, as portrayed in her final journey being towed up the Thames to be broken up for scrap in Turner's famous painting *The Fighting Temeraire*, today she sails triumphantly in her reborn splendour, a vision of magnificence in her original colours of gold and black.

The Temeraire had played a crucial role in achieving victory for Great Britain in the Battle of Trafalgar, and she was being celebrated on this day 200 years after that momentous and pivotal battle which sounded the death knell to Napoleon's ambitions of maritime conquest, when with elusive manoeuvres the elegant war ship thwarted the broadside musket fire and cannonballs with which Napoleon's befuddled soldiers sought to send her foundering to a watery grave.

Feeling the wind on my face, I reflect on more than three decades gone by since mother's navigation through perilous waters of institutionalised corruption back in our days of exile together, and on myself hitting the ground running from day one and going through the crucible of the British education system, making the transition from my secondary school tuition in Santa Marta to Tulse Hill School, a state comprehensive in the borough of Lambeth, south London. Fulfilling a lifelong ambition, and having completed studies in St Martin's School of Art and The College for the Distributive Trades, I became an independent art historian and gained a specialisation in the restoration and preservation of historic artworks.

As for mother, having been under the watchful eye of the witness protection programme for the best part of a year before my arrival, she slowly managed to pick up the pieces of her life, starting a new career working for the government's customs and immigration department at Heathrow Airport. She then went on to offering counselling and emotional support to women in prison, travelling on a weekly basis to Holloway Prison for women in London and to as far away as Greenock in the cold outreaches of Scotland, financing her long train journeys with her own personal resources. Her last occupation was caring for elderly residents in her community, until for health reasons, she had to stop, feeling she had given her all. Her hair was now as white as snow and her mobility severely restricted by joint pain and arthritis.

News had eventually reached us that our mentor and friend Marco Vinicio Suárez, with whom we exchanged correspondence on a regular basis had unexpectedly succumbed to a fatal heart attack just before I had completed my last year at school, an event that saddened me to the core of my being and which severed any meaningful connection with the life I had left behind. His passing also ended mother's hopes of averting the loss of her assets in Colombia, including farmland improperly absorbed in her absence and nationalised by the Colombian Institute for Agrarian Reform. Most remarkably, her career as a civil servant was erased from government records without explanation. After more than forty years, no amount of mediation through the consulate has yielded any formal acknowledgment of accountability from successive governments nor the will to activate a long-overdue pension for her seventeen-and-a-half years of public service.

Weather permitting, the light of day would often find me holding mother's hand for slow constitutional walks along Battersea Park and Kensington Gardens, the only outdoor leisure activity where she felt she could safely forego her ubiquitous walking stick.

During my work experience in the field of art and design, I was fortunate enough to be in the right city and in the right place to partake of a ground-breaking program of painting restoration, courtesy of the National Gallery's Scientific and Conservation Department. When news of work experience affording the opportunity to witness the restoration process on a certain Renaissance masterpiece reached my ears, I recalled the childhood feeling of swarms of butterflies in my stomach once more excitedly springing back into life.

"Sign me up for this", I pleaded with my tutor. "I will gladly serve tea and biscuits for the privilege."

Little by little, and through patient effort in the hands of curatorial staff, I watched centuries of grime and blackened varnish being painstakingly removed from the painting in a clockwise manner, unveiling the unvarnished truth for twenty-first-century eyes to see, the *magnum opus* appearing as clear and pristine as though it had just been given its finishing touches. In an upright position stood the original poplar panel of a painting that, in my primary school days, I had nicknamed 'The Virgin in the Cave', one of a plethora of images grandma kept in her room of private devotions in the yellow house, a depiction I now belatedly realised had been a poorly reproduced print of Leonardo da Vinci's *The Virgin of the Rocks*.

Walking through Kensington Gardens continues to bring me reminders of a distant past. Simple strolls down the streets of Chelsea frequently turn into educational events in which perennial myths from my childhood are deconstructed to their barest essentials, now standing revealed and demystified before me in their native environment. Conspicuous among them was Peter Pan, who had made such an indelible impression in my early years. The character, depicted by Disney as a ginger-haired youth with the gift of flight and a green costume adorned with leaves, may very well have been a historical figure known to posterity as Peter the Wild Boy, a lone feral boy who was discovered swinging from trees in a forest in Hanover by a party of hunters led by King George I. After his arrival in Britain, the boy was named Peter and adopted by the court at Kensington Palace. Peter's portrait can still be seen today in an eighteenth-century mural by William Kent, who designed and painted the palace's interiors, a mural which may well have served author J M Barrie – himself a frequent visitor of Kensington Palace – as inspiration for his literary version of Peter.

Every time I stopped to observe the dark bronze statue of the-boy-who-never-grew-up playing his pan pipes, I would compare the monument with my now dishevelled paper collage of Peter Pan, now some forty years old, which continued to fall apart every time I held it in my hands, a misshapen mess of fragments of coloured paper barely held together by vestiges of artisan glue. I marvelled at author J M Barrie's generous initiative in gifting

173

his copyright of Peter Pan to Great Ormond Street Hospital, to secure a future for sick children.

As for 'supercalifragilisticexpialidocious', that 'useful' word I had rigorously taught myself to recite until it stopped sounding like a tongue-twister was the only remnant of the legend of Mary Poppins that had persisted well into my adulthood. Wandering erratically around the Royal Borough of Kensington and Chelsea, I accidentally found my way to the unassuming brick house formerly inhabited by Pamela Lyndon Travers, creator of Mary Poppins.

A short bus ride from Chelsea would take me to Parliament Square, right in front of the real giant clock Georgiana had once drawn for me, where Peter first told Wendy "second to the right and straight on till morning".

I never quite persuaded my mother that the clock of Big Ben was five minutes too fast, as described in the novel, nor that the Banks family's make-believe house, 17 Cherry Tree Lane, occupied a non-existent half-moon-shaped street, complete with a weather vane to show the change in the direction of the wind. Upon reflection, I marvelled at the paradox of living in a world where fictitious characters such as the Banks could be deemed to have an imaginary fixed home address.

As for Georgiana, as much as I tried, I was never able to locate her actual address in Belgravia. Not long after the truth of her murder had become public knowledge, her parents set up a trust in her name through their solicitors, before relocating to Australia to further a lucrative business in a mining corporation. Ironically, it was far easier for me to find tangible evidence of popular myths dotted around the city of London than it was to find living proof that Georgiana had once been a real flesh-and-blood inhabitant of this world.

As I lay a single white lily in remembrance of her on the wrought-iron railing of a row of stucco-fronted terraced houses – any of which could well have been her residence, I reflect on the irony that, unlike imaginary characters such as Mary Poppins or Sherlock Holmes, Georgiana's brief passing through this life had left no visible imprint on the city of her birth.

And so it was that, just like the all-encompassing life-lesson revolving around the cycle of water that mother had instilled in me from an early age, I had finally come full circle from halcyon days of innocence when, under Caribbean skies, a boy with a boundless capacity for wonderment had constantly let his imagination soar in that big yellow house made of mud, craving spoonfuls of sugar and dreaming of finding Neverland.

I am brought back to the present by auspicious autumn winds, as if suddenly awakened from a dream, just in time to witness the majestic ship sailing across our field of vision towards the horizon, a lady veteran of a hundred wars.

There will be no ignoble end for her today.

Unlike in Turner's vision, the dazzling scene before our eyes is not the melancholy spectacle of a ghostly vessel symbolising the tragic breaking up of human life, nor the demise of a more heroic and graceful age that had forever been consigned to the distant past. Instead, mother and I look on at the setting sun over the Thames devoid of any fear, casting our eyes towards that place in the river where life's rich pageantry had begun once upon a time, placidly anticipating new beginnings from the ashes of the old world we had left behind, harbouring in our hearts the undying certainty of much brighter days yet to come.

ACKNOWLEDGEMENTS

Special thanks to Sandra Rocha Wilches for her unconditional love and support through the good and the bad times. I declare a huge debt of gratitude to Tom Wilson, my English tutor, for being a lasting inspiration and for never giving up on me while I was still struggling with the English language at Tulse Hill School, and to Andy Waterhouse, team leader at The Hut, for organising our school trips to France and Battersea Power Station while parts of it were still generating electricity for London. I remain grateful to the Stanton family for their hospitality and to Caroline Griffin for teaching me how to read poetry. My warmest gratitude to the wonderful Lotte Kashdan for introducing me to London's music scene and for granting me unfettered access to her valuable vinyl record collection. I thank John Gregg, my design teacher, for his vital support at Central St Martin's School of Art. Special acknowledgements to the following institutions: The National Gallery for providing me with work experience; The Victoria & Albert Museum for its unparalleled educational program and Historic Royal Palaces for its unique adult learning initiative. Acknowledgements to Manuel J. Diazgranados for his book "Geografía Económica del Magdalena", and to Jorge Enrique Elias Caro for his book "El Emprendimiento Industrial del Departamento del Magdalena (Colombia) en el Último Cuarto del Siglo XX". My deepest gratitude to Tabita Souto Miró for her timely advice and clarity of thought. Special thanks to Sonya Cristy for instilling in me a love of travel and above all for being an endless source of inspiration. To Candida Viveiros, for being my tower of strength in difficult times. I would like to acknowledge the efforts of McMillan Cancer Support and the extraordinary medical team at Catherine Lewis Centre in Hammersmith Hospital for nursing me back to health during eighteen months of chemotherapy treatment, a time I spent planning to write this book. And last but not least, special thanks to Carlos Martyn Burgos and Sandra Ospina for their practical support, kindness and generosity during the critical six months we were stranded abroad during the first year of the Covid pandemic.